Dear Reader,

Today we have a marriage revolution. The divorce revolution is over.

Men and women *want* to be married, want ceremonies with traditional bridal gowns, wedding parties and commitment. Formerly marrieds want remarriage, not with stereotyped husband and wife roles, but with self-determined roles.

In the 70's the emphasis was on the psychology of marriage, on personal adjustment, happiness and satisfaction—all concerns of the "me" generation.

In the 80's the emphasis is on the sociology of marriage. The new questions are: What is marriage? How do we divide it into its parts to better understand it? What can we do to make our marriages work?

How to Manage a Marriage encourages communication. Partners may be unable to discuss their ideas with each other because feelings and judgments get in the way. To facilitate talking between the partners, I have borrowed a concept from the law, a contract—The Listening Contract, a guarantee that each partner will be heard. It provides an orderly way to express opinions, ideas, judgments and feelings.

In this book you will hear from many marriage partners. Although their names are disguised, they live in print to share their experiences with you.

Marie Kargman

How to Manage a Marriage

How to Manage A Marriage

Marie Kargman

Published by Foundation Books

Boston, 1985

HQ10
.K33
1985x

For information: Foundation Books, 151 Tremont Street PH,
Boston, Massachusetts 02111.

Printed in the United States of America.

Library of Congress Catalog Number: 84-82624

ISBN 0-932477-00-3

To Max

My marriage partner since 1935

§

Contents

§

Introduction

What does a marriage counselor say to a client who makes an appointment, shows up, sits down in the chair, and says: "I don't want to be here. It's against everything I believe. We should be able to solve our own marriage problems."

Let me tell you what this marriage counselor says: "I agree, you should be able to work out your own marriage problems. *Let me teach you how.*"

For the past twenty-five years, hundreds of couples, some singly and some together, have come to share their troubled marriages with me. Many came asking me to save their marriages. I have never yet saved a marriage! I wouldn't know how to save someone else's marriage.

I have been teaching married couples, about-to-be-married couples, about-to-be-remarried couples, how to be their own marriage counselors. And for over forty years I have been trying to do what I teach others to do, namely to have and enjoy a husband-wife relationship that lives, expects, achieves, seeks goals, suffers, retrieves, rebuilds, and bathes itself in that balm of loving mutual respect.

MARRIED PEOPLE SAVE THEIR OWN MARRIAGES MANY TIMES DURING THE COURSE OF A LONG MARRIAGE. NO MARRIAGE STAYS AT THE SAME LEVEL OF CONTENTMENT FOREVER.

Can a Marriage Be Revived?

Yes, where there is a will to stay married. Marriage is a living relationship with cycles of dormancy and rebirth much like a perennial plant. Each partner can learn how to nourish the marriage so that it will bloom again. Couples come to me with troubled and wilted marriages that they desperately want to make well. I remember the Andersons, both in their early thirties, both successful in their careers, both wanting to stay married but wondering if it would be possible. "Even though we have fights," said John Anderson, "we still love each other. We really don't want a divorce, but we don't see any other ending for us if this keeps up. Help us before we stop loving each other."

Many times I have heard one spouse or the other say: "If we had come here ten years ago, there might have been some hope. But now it's too late for this marriage. We have grown so far apart, there is no love between us, there is nothing to revive. All we have now is bad memories, and we think that for everyone concerned, including the children, it would be best if we went ahead with a divorce."

Where love has been dead for too long, revival is very difficult. Impossible? Perhaps.

Divorce Is Discontinued Marriage

Divorce is a form of marriage. *It is ex-marriage.* And counseling for ex-marriage, for disengagement from the emotional survivals of a dead marriage, is more difficult on a how-to-do-it yourself program than is counseling yourself into a better marriage. Divorce counseling is a separate subject, not to be discussed in this book. Here we will concentrate on how to revive marriages that still have the will to live.

Forget Psychiatry!

You think you love each other, but you find it impossible to live together. When you are together it is nothing but argument. Could it be that you just weren't meant for each other? How do you know? At this point, many partners begin to think of psychiatric treatment. Forget psychiatry!

If you like your personality and you don't want to change, and your spouse likes his/her personality and doesn't want to change either, then perhaps you could learn to use your personalities differently. Using one's personality discriminatingly and changing it are very different. Psychiatry is for the individual. It can deal with depression, compulsion, rigidity, frigidity, personality highs and lows. It always focuses on the person.

Marriage counseling focuses on the relationship. It is always concerned with two people, never one. It is always concerned with specific occurrences in time and place. It doesn't deal with attitudes, it deals with behavior. Marriage counseling helps husband and wife to look at what started an argument or conflict and what responses were made. A stormy marriage does not necessarily mean you need psychiatry. Many marriage partners with good mental health have marital problems. Such marital problems, unresolved, lead to disappointments, frustrations, and emotional outbursts. If the marital problem is the source of the trouble and not your personality, you don't need psychiatry.

You Can Counsel Yourself to a Better Marriage

You begin your own marriage counseling by asking yourself, "What can I do to help this marriage?" There is never just one answer. You will explore a variety of possible answers and communicate them to your spouse. Together you will test their appropriateness, eliminate the answers that you both agree are not possible, devise ways to experiment with the probable answers, and take responsibility for a particular new way of taking care of an old problem. Each partner must ask how he or she expects to participate in the counseling process.

Remember, the focus is "What can *I* do?"—as distinguished from the more usual way that partners talk to each other, saying "What I want from *you* is . . ."

One

§

You Can Be Your Own Marriage Counselor

If your marriage is not as happy as it could be, this book will teach you how to counsel yourself into a better one. If you have a happy marriage, this book will help to make it even stronger. But what is marriage? We seldom stop to analyze something so common!

Marriage Is Relationship

If you think of *husband-wife* as just one pairing relationship among many other familiar relationships, like landlord-tenant, buyer-seller, employer-worker, lawyer-client, doctor-patient, and architect-builder, then it will perhaps become clear that marriage counseling involves problems common to all pair relationships. Differences in expectations and performance, understandings and misunderstandings, are built into all pair relationships.

GIVE YOURSELVES THE CHANCE TO STRAIGHTEN OUT THE RE-
LATIONSHIP WHILE YOU ARE STILL HEALTHY ENOUGH TO LOOK
AT EACH OTHER AND SEE THE PROBLEMS BETWEEN YOU, NOT
WITHIN EACH ONE OF YOU SEPARATELY.

Marriage Is Respect

Each partner must first have self-respect. Self-respect
helps you to listen to what your partner is saying, even
though you might not like what you are hearing. Without
self-respect you cannot listen to criticism because the
natural impulse is to interrupt and defend yourself or to
retreat into self-pity. *Self-respect is the foundation for
good listening.*

No marriage can be good unless both partners listen to
each other. Listening nurtures mutual respect. The partner
who doesn't respect himself or herself cannot participate
in marriage counseling. Where does one get self-respect?
Self-respect is self-taught; you learn to respect yourself
just as you learn not to respect yourself.

Marriage partners can learn to develop self-respect and,
even more important, how to recognize when they don't
have self-respect. You will share, in this book, the experiences of partners who went through the process of finding
ways to talk to each other respectfully.

Marriage Is Talk

Every marriage is ideally an agreement for respectful exchange at all levels of communication—through

words, touch, sex, sight, and hearing.

Many partners wrongfully believe that marriage gives them the right to say anything they please to each other at any time.

Marriage counseling is not helpful if you don't know how to talk to each other. How to acquire the patience to listen without interrupting; how to interrupt with permission; how to communicate a negative feeling without arousing hostility; how to ask for love, sympathy, and affection and get it; all of these skills come from understanding and using a marriage-communication tool called *the listening contract.*

A listening contract will help you to minimize the risk *inherent in every conversation,* and especially between husband and wife, of being misunderstood. Every exchange of words has three possible levels of simultaneous understanding—the *idea,* the *feeling,* and the *judgment.* Words state facts, they express emotion, and they convey decisions of right and wrong, good and bad, and likes and dislikes. Once partners learn to recognize the complexities of language, that one simple sentence can be interpreted on three levels and is never free of several meanings, partners are more willing to listen to the language used in communication instead of assuming they "know" what the other is talking about. Good listening makes for better talk between marriage partners. A listening contract prevents bad talk, destructive words, and unhappy feelings. If your marriage suffers from misunderstandings in communication, look to Chapter Two, "The Listening Contract," for help.

Marriage Is a Social Organization

Marriage has an intricate social structure. Each new marriage creates a new family of two people with two new titles, namely "husband" and "wife." In this new family husband and wife are free to make any internal arrangements they wish, limited only by the laws of the government under which they live. Governments try to interfere as little as possible in the internal structure of this new family. Yet, as soon as husband and wife begin their married lives within the new unit they have created, they begin to feel the pressure of expectations. Their new society expects that certain tasks—like housework—will be performed, and suddenly the partners discover that marriage has a structure. There are new boundaries to their freedom. They are now part of an organization, a social organization called "marriage."

Every marriage is a social organization made up of three systems:

Marriage is a political system—a mini-government involving power and authority, rights and obligations. Marriage partners often try to use their power to impose their own rules on each other. Chapter Three will help you to learn to share authority without competing for power.

Marriage is an economic system—a mini-business involving money, time, and services. A good marriage is a partnership, not an employer-employee relationship. Chapter Four helps you deal with the "business" of being married.

Marriage is a kinship system—a mini-society which

creates ties between the spouses and their relatives. Kinship ritual and expectations can create confusion and cause tension. Look to Chapter Five for help in improving the kinship network.

Marriage Is Expectations

The political system, the economic system, and the kinship system, in other words, the rules for sharing power, goods, services, and family members, all create expectations in each partner—expectations of what each must do and what each will get. Unfulfilled expectations lead to disappointment, unhappiness, and a tendency to be hostile to the one who has defaulted.

Some couples fail to examine their mutual expectations for inconsistencies and are unfair to each other. Too often partners attack each other instead of attacking the marriage problem which results from one or more of the systems. Some marriage partners choose to label all emotional expressions of disappointment as personality disturbances.

We must try to relate the disappointment to the expectation. If the disappointment can be avoided by rearranging our expectations, there will be fewer emotional outbursts. When marriage partners know that there are specific differences in what each expects of the other as well as what each expects of himself or herself, then they can begin to sort the differences they can live with from the differences that must be resolved in some way.

Sometimes conflicting expectations involve sex. For some insights into sexual expectations in marriage, see Chapter Six.

Marriage Is Finding the Alternatives

Two people can, in all good faith, see a particular difference and its resolution in two totally different ways, and each be "right." We are each a product of our own family history and we have the tendency to defend the concepts and ideas we learned as children; they are familiar and comfortable. But again, no two people have the same family experience. Except in very rare instances there is no "right" or "wrong" way to resolve a marital problem.

There are always alternatives; some are better than others. Sometimes one of the partners uses an extramarital affair as an alternative to marital problems. See Chapter Seven for some new perspectives on an old problem.

Partners can only learn which alternatives are better for them if they make as careful an analysis of the problem as is possible. Finding alternatives is the key to changing disturbing behavior in marriage. There is never just one way! And that is what Chapter Eight, "Nine Handles for Marriage Managers," is all about.

Marriage Is Challenge

Every marriage has challenges. Some people call them problems. Problems and their solutions can disrupt a marriage or enhance it.

Every marriage has conflict. Conflict can be trouble or fun. What you do about your problems, how you talk about them to your spouse—the tone of voice, the gestures, the emotional overtones of conversation, the accusations, the apologies—is all part of the challenge of marriage.

Since it is not possible to learn how to be married until you *are* married, every marriage needs adjustments. Partners need to learn how to talk about making adjustments, lest one partner presume to counsel the other. Such presumption is an abuse of power and seldom tolerated.

Therefore, *don't try to be a marriage counselor to your spouse*. Counsel yourself, know your marriage, know the differences you can learn to live with and those you can't. When necessary, ask for a listening contract to discuss alternative solutions you have to offer.

Within the life-space of marriage two people can find personal fulfillment, happiness, psychological security, contentment, personal growth, psychological relaxation, physical relaxation, sexual satisfaction, and every positive state known to man. You will find you *can* be your own marriage counselor and reap all the rewards of a good marriage.

Two

§

The Listening Contract

Words and eggs must be handled with care.
Once broken they are impossible things to repair.
Anne Sexton

When You Need a Listening Contract

When your marriage is troubled and you don't talk to each other, then you need a listening contract.

When you argue all the time, then you need a listening contract.

When you complain that "no one ever listens to me," then you need a listening contract.

When you pray for the day that your spouse will let you finish a sentence without interrupting you, then you need a listening contract.

When your spouse is always "translating" or telling other people what you meant by what you said, then you need a listening contract.

When you say, after ten years of marriage, "there is nothing to talk about," then you need a listening contract.

When your spouse always changes the subject when you begin to talk, then you need a listening contract.

A LISTENING CONTRACT IS A COUNSELING TOOL FOR HUSBANDS AND WIVES, WHO, HAVING LOST THEIR WILLINGNESS TO LISTEN TO EACH OTHER, AGREE TO REESTABLISH A LISTENING RELATIONSHIP.

Does "Listen To Me!" Mean "Do As I Tell You!"

Bill York is a New York stockbroker who was never handy with his hands, rarely fixed anything because he never had to in the apartment building where he lived as a bachelor, who took the plunge and moved into a house in the suburbs. He said that almost each Friday, at the beginning of the weekend, when he arrived home, his wife Betty would greet him with a kiss and a hug and say, " . . . and these are the jobs that need to be done this weekend." He used to listen, but then he discovered that Betty would get upset when, after listening to her read the list—put up the shelves in the cellar, fix the lock on the bathroom door, take the mower to the repair shop (all of which made him tired before the weekend started, he said)—he would do the jobs he had planned for *himself*. If his list and Betty's list were different, Betty acted as though she had been betrayed by Bill. After all, he did listen, so why didn't he do the things he heard she had planned for him?

Bill was willing to listen so long as the list of things for him to do was a suggestion, something for them to talk about, the subject for conversation and information. But when he began to feel that listening created promises in Betty's mind, never intended by Bill, he could no longer allow himself to listen. It created unnecessary problems, he thought. He thought if he didn't listen, then he wouldn't have the obligation to do all the tasks Betty had lined up. Betty lost Bill as a listener. Why?

To Bill the word "listen" means "to give close attention with the purpose of hearing." To Betty the word "listen" means "to yield to advice." According to Webster's New International Dictionary, both are acceptable meanings.

Which Meaning Increases Communication Between Spouses?

Bill York is a good example of what happens to listening when listening means "to yield to advice." If listening carries an obligation to *do* what the talker is advising, why listen? Why be obligated? It is no wonder then that so many husbands and wives have stopped listening to each other. As for Betty York, her response when Bill failed to do all the tasks he had heard her talk about was, "Why should I waste my breath talking to him? My advice is never followed. He just does what *he* wants to do."

Betty's definition of listening discourages communication. As Bill discovered, listening can be hazardous! Who knows what commitments he would be obligated to make just by listening?

"But how do I get Bill to fix things around the

house?" asked Betty. "He won't even *hear* me anymore."

The real question Betty is asking is: How do you get another person to do something you want them to do? The quick answer is: You don't.

If Betty could change her question to "How can I motivate Bill to want to do the tasks I have told him need to be done?" she would be on the road to an enriching communication experience.

WITHOUT TALKING AND LISTENING, NO MARRIAGE CAN EXIST. "TO GIVE CLOSE ATTENTION WITH THE PURPOSE OF HEARING"– AND ONLY HEARING–MUST BE THE MEANING OF LISTENING.

Bill and Betty need a listening contract. They must open the way for talk without commitment to do.

The fun in marriage comes from dreams, hopes, crazy ideas—all discussed in a climate of affection where the partners can relax with each other because nothing else but attention is asked. A new trust is established, one which says, "by listening to me, you incur no obligations." Each partner hopes the other will want to listen and perhaps even follow some of the suggestions offered. With this attitude there is no risk of disappointment turning to anger.

Every Exchange of Talk Is a Potential Source of Conflict

Contrary to what many married partners believe, marriage itself is not an obligation to be always available for listening.

Two marriage partners, each with a different point of view about a particular occurence (an incident or conflict), can learn to talk to each other with respect. Lack of respect and the breakdown of the husband-wife relationship come from not knowing the complexity of exchange between a "talker" (the initiator of a particular conversation) and a "listener."

The most simple statement between husband and wife can never be simple, because every communication between husband and wife takes place simultaneously on three levels of understanding. Each verbal act (talking is a verbal act) *sends* a message along three communications pathways: (1) the *idea* path, a thinking process; (2) the *feeling* path, an emotional process; and (3) the *judgment* path, a moral process. And each verbal message is *received* on all three pathways of idea, feeling, and judgment. Thus a single spoken sentence can elicit any one of nine possible responses with eight possibilities for misunderstanding.

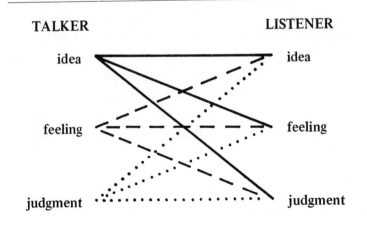

Since the listener must choose to open the response with one out of the possible nine replies, the chance for error is great. While a listener might be aware of many possible replies, an individual can only talk about one level at a time.

Let us discuss the dilemma of one couple, Jack and Susan Adams. Susan says, "You didn't pick me up when you said you would." Did she mean she was wondering *why* her husband was delayed? Or she was *annoyed* because she was kept waiting? Or is he a *liar,* who never keeps his word? Jack replies on the idea level: "The car didn't work and I had no way to contact you." If he guessed right, the partners had a respectful communication. She wanted to know *why,* he told her, she was satisfied, and that unit of interaction was over. *Why* is a request on the idea level. But if Susan was *annoyed* with Jack for being late and expected him to respond to her feelings of unhappiness, an answer about the condition of the car would be no answer at all.

What could Jack say to show that he got the feeling message? He could say, "You are annoyed with me for being late and I don't blame you." While it might not satisfy Susan's unhappiness, it would, from a communications point of view, put both talker and listener on the same wavelength. But if Susan was telling Jack that he never keeps his word, then Jack would be obligated to reply with words that told Susan he was aware of her judgment, that he hears it.

Now you can see why it is not uncommon for marriage partners to discover they aren't talking about the same subject, or on the same level.

The Commitments of Listening

Listening is a commitment to hear with the ears, to see with the eyes, to feel every touch, and smell every scent. It is total attention. Listening is a promise to refrain from thinking "What will I say back?" while one partner is talking. In each listening contract there is still another promise: I promise not to interrupt while you are talking and you promise not to interrupt when it is my turn to talk.

Mature listening is not easy. Although Doris Lawrence said she was ready to listen to her husband talk about why he had left her, she made faces while he was talking, as if to say, "I don't believe you." She smoked cigarette after cigarette, making the lighting of each cigarette a dramatic event; she moved her lips to form the words "liar," and she whispered negativisms under her breath when her husband said, "I am a good father."

Doris wanted another chance to listen after I pointed out her "nonlistening" behavior. David Lawrence agreed to retell his story so that Doris could hear not only the facts, but his feelings and the judgments he was making about her and himself. Although Doris thought she was ready to listen the first time, she found she was not.

When I asked Doris, "Tell me what you heard your husband say," she said, "He said I'm no good, I'm a poor housekeeper." "Did you hear any of his sadness, anger, happiness, love?" She shook her head from side to side. "You only heard the bad things he said about you. Did you hear him say anything bad about himself?" Again, she shook her head from side to side.

Undoubtedly, Doris and David Lawrence were unable

to talk to each other in their own home without each encounter ending in a serious quarrel. Could the cycle be
stopped? Could they learn to contract to listen to each
other? How could I help them?

Preparation for the Listening Contract

Since the goal of this book is to give you the tools for
doing at home what clients do in the professional counselor's office, I must tell you how I orient the client to
the professional counseling session.

When the partners come together, I tell them: "I must
do whatever I can to make this meeting a meaningful experience and not a repetition of the quarreling that goes on
between you when I am not present." I say I expect disagreement, but controlled disagreement. Then I tell them
the ground rules.

Both partners will get a chance to talk. Interruptions,
except for *symbolic interrupters,* will not be tolerated because they prevent us from hearing the completion of
an idea or thought. Some wise man once said, "A good
listener is not only popular everywhere, but after a while
he knows something."

Each partner will have the opportunity to give a personal interpretation of the same conflict. In this way we
will all hear the differences.

If one of the partners cannot refrain from interrupting,
that partner must ask permission to disrupt before making
a statement. If permission is granted, the interruption will

be permitted; if not granted, the disruptor will have to wait for the proper time to speak.

Sometimes couples who haven't laughed together for a long time find themselves so unaccustomed to asking permission to interrupt, that looking at each other learning to restrain impulsive behavior causes them to laugh.

Sometimes lawyers who send clients to me say, "Are you sure you want them to come together?" So often, partners who have been advised by their lawyers not to communicate with each other directly appreciate the opportunity to talk in a controlled environment. The lawyer's advice was based upon their experiences in a conventional legal conference. In the proper communication climate, even emotionally charged clients can learn to have a meaningful listening contract.

Guidelines for Making Your Own Listening-Contract Climate

IF YOU WANT TO HAVE A MEETING WITH YOUR PARTNER, AND YOU BOTH KNOW THAT EVERY MEETING ENDS IN A QUARREL, *YOU* HAVE THE OBLIGATION TO MAKE IT CLEAR TO YOUR PARTNER THAT YOU ACCEPT THE RESPONSIBILITY FOR MAKING THIS MEETING DIFFERENT.

1. Tell your partner you know that every time you have asked for a talk, it hasn't turned out well. Assume responsibility for the way the last quarrel turned out—i.e., "I kept interrupting you, but this time I want a chance to

show you that I can refrain from interrupting."

2. Try to accept suggestions for procedure. If your spouse says, "This is your idea so tell me first what you intend to do," accept this recommendation. Since the meeting is at your request, *you* must be prepared to *tell* your story, to be the narrator.

3. Don't ask questions of your spouse. *Asking questions is not telling a story.* The initiating partner who asks questions instead of telling must be prepared to face the question: "Why should I answer you?" To avoid this confrontation before the partners are ready to handle disagreement, it is imperative that the partner who initiates the conference for preparing a listening contract refrain from asking questions. For example: The question "Why did you come home so late?" may lead to unforeseen trouble. Whereas the statement, "I was worried about you last night, I thought something might have happened to you," tells the speaker's concern. For a fuller discussion of questions, listen to Mr. and Mrs. S in Chapter Five.

For many marriage partners this guideline is the most difficult one to follow. To ask a question is to place the burden of telling and going forward with the meeting on the listener. This is not the contract. The initial burden must be on the partner who is seeking to make a listening contract. The initiating partner must be the "talker" and must begin the communication with a statement of fact, feeling, or judgment.

4. Recommend a *symbolic interrupter.* Partners planning to negotiate a listening contract will undoubtedly feel the need to interrupt each other. It is unrealistic to assume that old patterns of conflict will be contained.

The symbolic interrupter is an agreed-upon word, symbol, or sign that can be used by either party, which says, "Let's stop here for a moment, I think we are headed for trouble."

The partners also agree that when the symbolic interrupter is used, they will stop to analyze where they got off the communications track.

The use of the symbolic interrupter avoids any need by either partner to *explain why* the decision to interrupt was made at that time. The partners just agree in advance to stop and not to question the decision. They have decided to take the place of the professional marriage counselor by monitoring their own communications.

A symbolic interrupter can be a gesture of the hand, the wave of a handkerchief, or just a word. When Watergate was a household noun, it was a popular symbol that meant trouble ahead.

5. Try to be accepting. It is easier to listen to compliments and neutral talk than to negative criticism. Negativism turns the listener off. Unless the partners agree that they want to learn to tolerate negative criticism as part of the climate for a listening contract, beware of being a self-appointed critic.

Accept the idea that two people can, in good faith, look at the same circumstances and have two different conclusions or opinions. State your opinion without being critical of your partner.

6. Experiment with learning alternative ways to express yourself. There is never just one way to express an idea, a feeling, or a judgment. The partner who feels misjudged might psychologically leave the conversation. If

you find yourself judging your partner, saying "You're wrong," try instead to tell how you feel. Say: "I don't like what I hear."

By placing the responsibility on yourself, you now can clarify what you heard. "I heard you say . . . when I thought that what happened was . . . The difference I see is . . . " The suggested alternative encourages more exploration between the partners.

7. Never request a meeting to give advice. The partner who presumes to give advice claims a position of power. (See Chapter Three.) No partner likes to be told, "I know more than you, therefore I am telling you."

Even if your partner should ask you for advice, be careful. Such requests sometimes mask a strong desire for talk on a *feeling* level or a counterrequest: "Ask me for advice." If you are unsure of how to respond to a request for advice, you, the partner who wants to keep the climate open for communication, must try to explore further the request for advice. For example, Mr. A wants to have a meeting to explore a listening contract about child discipline. Mrs. A says, "Do you think I should tell Sue to be home at ten o'clock?" Mr. A's first impulse is to tell Mrs. A what to do. But uncertain that Mrs. A is actually asking for that, he says, "You sound like you are not sure this is the right thing to say. Let's talk about it . . ." Thus, Mrs. A, if she has feelings about what she should say to their daughter, will have an oportunity to discuss them.

8. Avoid responding to a *feeling* communication with a self-reference. Most partners who ask for a listening contract to have a discussion of feelings want support and sympathy or even empathy for the hurt expressed. If your

partner tells you what a terrible day it was, how awful people were, how many interruptions there were, don't say, "You think that's bad. You should have had my day and then you would know how lucky you are." Comparing or measuring feelings doesn't help the partner who wants to hear, "It sounds like a really bad day. You must have suffered."

If the partner who wants sympathy could recognize that what is about to be said might be called "bitching," that partner might tell the listener, "I feel very bitchy today. Please, just listen to me bitch. You don't have to answer. I don't expect you to do anything about it."

A listening contract sets up a procedure for handling formerly troublesome marital problems, one at a time. Each problem must have a separate contract. If partners use these guidelines to prepare themselves for a listening contract, then deciding the terms of the contract can be an exploration in "togetherness."

Role Expectations Are Silent Messages

As the bride and groom grow into their roles of husband and wife, they learn what each expects of the other. In a healthy marriage the couple establishes a family culture and their communications often include words unspoken but understood by them. But in troubled marriages those unspoken words increase misunderstandings.

Let's explore. Husband Joe says, "My suit needs cleaning." Wife Jane hears this statement but does not respond. What are Jane's risks for future misunderstanding? Jane says, "I run no risks. He didn't ask me to do anything about his suit that needed cleaning." Was Joe asking Jane to take his suit to the cleaners even though he did not put his words in the form of a question? Does Jane wonder why Joe told her about his dirty suit? Does Jane wonder enough to ask, "Joe, are you asking me to take your suit to the cleaners?" This would clarify her uncertainty, if she had any questions in her mind. And what about Joe? I have known many Joes who, under these circumstances, would say, "Why do you think I was telling her my suit needs cleaning?" These Joes assume they have a right to ask their wives to take care of cleaning chores as a part of their marriage contract. Whether Jane sees the marriage contract as defining role obligations too we could only guess. If she took the suit to the cleaners, it might well be that she understood. Since the case is hypothetical, we could guess that Joe never intended Jane to do anything for him by his statement. If Jane did, it might be because of her own sexist conditioning.

In today's climate of changing role expectations, partners who do services for each other might reject the idea that they are establishing expected patterns. The new equality between the sexes within the family seems to require more clarification of communication, since both partners want to be sure that cultural conditioning is not interfering with their understanding of each other.

When husbands and wives say, "It is not just one thing but many little things added together that make trouble for us," they are expressing the frustration of learning the magnitude of husband-wife expectation.

Since faulty communication is the number one cause

of marital breakdown, according to the Family Service Association of America, the do-it-yourself marriage counselor is advised to look at the *quality of listening* in his or her marriage.

When you are a listener, try to get a reading on what the talker intends and expects. Satisfy yourself that you understand the *idea* of the message, the *emotion* of the message, and the *judgment* of the message. If you are not sure what the talker expects of you, your chance of making a right decision is better if you ask for clarification. Tell your spouse what you believe the three possibilities are and then choose the one you think is most appropriate.

In the same manner, if you are the talker who is not being understood, try to give the listener more discriminating clues. Don't expect the listener to know unless you tell.

Is such deliberate communication possible between marriage partners who are having trouble? A listening contract will provide the climate within which such deliberation is expected behavior.

The "Not Listening" Complaint

Mr. Sharp complained, "My wife never listens to me." When I asked Mr. Sharp to rephrase his attack upon his wife so that she might be encouraged to listen, he said, "I don't like the way she answers me."

Mr. Sharp is a businessman. His complaint is one I have heard from many businessmen.

A husband might tell his wife about a business decision he has to make. He is worried about it. And the wife will give him a quick solution without considering whether or not she is qualified to do so. Very often this wife knows very little about the intricacies of the business. The quick reply makes her husband angry and she doesn't know why. To her, she was only answering his question.

This husband was not asking his wife to solve his business problem. The business problem was the *idea* in his conversation. He really wanted to talk about his *emotional* upset over having the problem. What he hoped for from his wife was a sympathetic or empathetic expression about the difficulties he faces in "making a living." He wanted her to be aware of how hard his day is and he wanted her to let him know that she understands.

He accuses her of not listening because she didn't tell him she *heard* his feelings of unhappiness. He is angry and he says to her, "You sure do have all the answers, don't you?" (Referring to her solution to his problem in business.)

The wife now feels attacked and says, "What are you so mad about? I only wanted to help." She tries to pick up the idea of anger and wants to discuss it. (She did not respond in anger.)

Her husband says, "You help? What do you know about business?"

Mr. Sharp, like other husbands in this situation, resents his wife's presumption that she could have an answer for his troublesome business problem, when he, who is more expert, doesn't. He sees his wife's solution as a challenge to him; and the marriage partners, without intending, find themselves in a contest over who has the right answer.

Marriage partners can avoid this business pitfall if they remember that most husbands who complain about having to make a difficult decision are not asking their wives, nor do they want their wives, to solve their business problems. These husbands are asking for sympathy or sometimes just want to let off a little steam, asking for no response at all. If a wife wants to answer, she would be safer addressing herself to the *feeling* and not the *idea*. She might say, "You have many hard decisions to make, it takes a lot out of you." This would give the husband an opportunity to continue to talk about his feelings if he wants to. He might then be encouraged by his wife to talk about the *idea* of the problem. This will come about in the course of the conversation. In my experience, after the husband is sure his wife understands how difficult things are for him, he is willing to talk about the *idea* element of his problems.

Mr. and Mrs. Sharp decided to make a listening contract about "business talk" at home. Mrs. Sharp wanted to know how to talk about business without Mr. Sharp feeling that his judgments were being attacked. They agreed that whenever Mr. Sharp did feel attacked they would use a symbolic interrupter and then talk about the introduction of anger into a conversation that both partners wanted to keep on the *idea* level.

"Not listening" complaints come from wives too. Another common complaint concerns the partner in the driver's seat of an automobile.

Mrs. Lloyd said, "He does this to me all the time. I

had to ask him the same question three times before he would answer me."

Mr. Lloyd said, "My wife doesn't believe me when I tell her I don't hear her asking me questions when I am driving the car."

Mrs. Lloyd said, "I am sitting right next to him. If he doesn't hear me, it is because he doesn't want to."

I asked the Lloyds to reenact in the office their last argument over driving in the car.

When Mrs. Lloyd expressed anger because she assumed Mr. Lloyd heard her and didn't answer, I asked her how she could have verified her *judgment* that he didn't want to answer her before she got angry.

She said, "I could have asked 'Are you hearing me?' or I guess I could even have poked him and said, 'I want you to listen to me.'"

Mr. Lloyd said, "When we are in the car, my wife is always talking. She says so many things. Sometimes I get so involved in my own thoughts I don't even know she is talking."

Mrs. Lloyd said, "That is what makes me mad. He should be listening to me."

Now I asked Mr. Lloyd if he felt that he should always be listening.

Here was an expressed difference in their expectations of each other in the car.

The Lloyds decided to make a listening contract about car communication. Mr. Lloyd agreed that he would be available for listening in the car, but that Mrs. Lloyd would have to give him better clues that she was talking since self-involvement and driving prevented him from looking at her. She agreed to use not only her voice, but to touch him if she thought he needed further clues.

Mrs. Lloyd was reluctant to make a contract for this problem. But Mr. Lloyd wanted a contract because he was very much bothered by the arguments they had while driving. Why? "Because we usually get out of the car angry and the rest of the day is spoiled," he said.

Mr. Lloyd agreed there was carry-over and for that reason it was important to have the listening contract and especially the symbolic interrupters.

Mrs. Lloyd particularly objected to all my suggestions about giving her husband clues. "Is all that necessary?" she asked.

I told her when a particular pattern of communication has been established over a long period of time, it would be more difficult to change than if it were a recent problem. Learning to deal with an old problem takes more direct, simple language and clues in order to establish change.

Learning to communicate in a relationship that has a long history of explosive interaction is like learning to read each other in a new way; very deliberate observation of one's self is required as well as observation of the partner. The symbolic interrupters, agreed upon in advance, prevent the partners from adding further trouble in deciding when to interrupt. They make interruption noncompetitive.

Eventually, when new patterns are learned, they become just as automatic as the old ones, and the partners again have a new family shorthand with built-in respect for all the members.

Both examples of "not listening" above were concerned with verbal communication: Not listening can be a nonverbal complaint too.

The wife of a law student lamented that her husband didn't love her any more and she knew this because when she put her arms around him, he pushed her away.

I said to her, "Tell me, what was your husband doing when you put your arms around him?"

"He was studying," she said.

In the moment following her answer to me, as though simply saying, "He was studying," had caused her to rethink the whole incident about which she was complaining, she said in a very apologetic voice, "I only wanted him to know how much I love him."

Her voice suggested that perhaps her message didn't get across and she was wondering whether, if she did it again, she should do what she did differently. What could I suggest?

"Rethink the episode," I suggested. "Would you consider putting your arms around your husband when he is studying an interruption on a nonverbal level?"

"Telling him I love him is an interruption?" she asked. And, after another moment, she talked again. "Could it be?"

"If you think of the 'expectations' in this encounter, would you say there might be some conflict in expectations?" I hinted.

"I expected him to take my hug as an act of love. I suppose he took my hug as an interference with his studying. He probably expected me to respect his studying privacy. Should I not hug him when I want to?" she asked.

"To avoid a misunderstanding, and to make sure that he should expect an act of love and not an interference, perhaps you could ask for permission to interrupt the studying and tell him why," was my response.

This wife and her student husband entered into a listening contract setting down expectations for "study interruption." A provision within the contract reads: I agree that sometimes when I try to put my arms around you I am a little jealous of all the time you spend studying. I need to be reassured that you love me and therefore I hope you will hug me instead of pushing me away.

Her husband agreed that he would try to remember not to be annoyed at the interruption but respond to the love that is intended.

I advised the wife that if sometimes she should hug her husband as a surprise and if he didn't push her away but didn't hug her either, that instead of being disappointed that there was no action on his part, she look upon the incident as follows: You want to hug your husband. That is your goal. That is your expectation—an opportunity to put your arms around him. You put your arms around him. You fulfilled your expectation. If you don't expect your husband to do something in return, but only to receive, then you won't be disappointed.

She understood that *very often we create our own disappointments by making our happiness depend upon something we want other people to do.* If each partner could learn to expect disappointment as a possibility and not be surprised by it, disappointment within the communication system could be seen as an *idea*. If the wife says to herself, "I'll hug him and if he doesn't hug me back, I won't be angry because I will feel good after the hug," and if she feels a tinge of anger when her husband doesn't respond, she can then discuss with herself—as an idea, an intellectual process—her own anger. "Why am I angry?"

In discussing the terms of their listening contract, the wife agreed that if she did get angry, she would look to herself to understand her anger and not accuse her husband of "making me mad," as she had previously done. He, on the other hand, agreed to recognize his wife's need for more affection.

What Do We Talk About? We Don't Know Each Other

Mr. and Mrs. Argum have been married fifteen years. Mr. Argum is a consultant and travels a good deal. He is usually home on weekends only. Mrs. Argum looks forward to his coming home and then she suffers all weekend because all the conversations she dreamed she would have with her husband over the weekend just never take place. She wants to know why.

Mr. Argum says, "I'll tell her anything she wants to know."

What's wrong here?

Mrs. Argum is expressing an emotional frustration, undefined, about her inability to have a close relationship with her husband. She wants to have many things to talk about and finds she has little to say. Her attempts to make conversation with her husband are short-lived because when she says, "Did you have a good trip?" he answers, "Yes." End of conversation!

"Did you think about us all last week?"

"Yes." End of conversation.

What could Mrs. Argum do to help herself?

First, she must accept the idea that Mr. Argum is not an easy person to talk with; he does not volunteer information.

Second, since she is the one who wants to change the present situation, she must ask herself, "How do *I* become a better conversationalist?"

Third, she should ask herself, "What can I do or say that would encourage my husband to want to tell me more and pay more attention to me?"

Mrs. Argum asked her husband for a listening contract. She asked him to listen to her need for a closer relationship. She agreed that when he came home she would talk for the first five minutes about her week at home, including what the children did, but excluding asking her husband to punish the children. (Mr. Argum said they did at one time talk about the children, but he grew tired of hearing about how bad they were and how difficult it was without him home.)

Mr. Argum agreed not to answer questions with a "Yes" or "No," but would answer with at least a simple sentence of description.

Mr. and Mrs. Argum each agreed to make a list of subjects they would like to learn to talk about with each other.

Then, by trial and error, they would play talking games for designated periods of time.

Mrs. Argum agreed to help Mr. Argum by encouraging him with such words as "Tell me more ... " and "Would you like to tell me what you said when ... " She also agreed to try sending Mr. Argum small notes through the mail about the children and their activities so they could have details to talk about, i.e., "Johnny made a goal in hockey on Tuesday. You should have seen him take the puck away from ... " This gives Mr. Argum a chance to say, "Tell me more about the hockey game."

Some Things to Remember About Listening Contracts

1. A listening contract is tailored to a specific marital trouble.

2. It offers the marriage partners an opportunity to learn to change old habits that create problems for the partners.

3. It makes trial and error a new way to find a solution to an old problem.

4. It presumes that both partners understand the complex nature of talking and listening and the built-in chances of error in understanding.

5. It offers the partners a way to stop themselves from being negative through the use of the symbolic interrupter.

6. It says the established patterns of interaction be-

tween the partners were learned. New ways can be learned too.

7. When the new ideas become old ideas, a family culture or shorthand will develop. The listening contract is the tool to help you get from "the way it was" to "what we want for our marriage."

Three

§

Marriage Is
a Political System

*There is little less trouble in governing
a private family than a whole kingdom.*
Montaigne

A family is a small new state. Families, like other political states, must have laws that distribute rights and obligations among family members. As is true of other political
structures, conflicts come when the marriage partners are
not clear about what is expected of them and what they
owe to others outside the marriage. Some marriage partners disagree on what the rules in their family are and each
one looks for the right to make his or her own interpretation. Some marriage partners, even though they know the
established "law" of their marriage, choose not to abide by
it. Like political states, families must make some arrangements for deciding how rules are to be made, who is responsible for executing them, and what is to be done when
the marriage partners differ.

WHEN MARRIAGE PARTNERS FEEL THAT DEMOCRACY DOES NOT EXIST IN THEIR MARRIAGE, THEY COMPETE FOR THE POWER TO BE MORE POWERFUL.

Argument in a marriage is usually competition for the power to impose their own opinion upon the other partner. Husbands and wives rarely stop to ask themselves, "What is the rule of law in this family on this issue?" or "What form of government do we have—a democracy or a kingdom?" Most married people bring into marriage the attitudes and rules in the families in which they grew up. Coming to agreement is marriage work.

Ask yourself the question: How is my family governed? Can you give an answer? Let's look at how Sally and Larry learned to establish their family government:

"Sally and I went marketing at the Stop and Shop," said Larry, a newlywed who was still a student and very limited financially. "Sally works all week, and since I'm at school and then go to work, I take the car to school. On Friday night I don't work and so we decided to do the marketing together. We were walking down one of the aisles when I saw a box of cookies and threw them into the basket. Sally just took the box and put it back on the shelf. She said, 'We can't afford it; it isn't in the budget.'

"I said, 'But I want them.'

"She replied, 'But you cannot have them. I worked this budget over very carefully. We only buy what is on this list.'

"'This box goes back in the basket,' I said. 'Don't tell me I can't have a box of cookies for sixty-nine cents, if I want it.'

" 'You can't have them,' she said. 'If you break the budget here, you'll break it someplace else and then all my planning might just as well be thrown out the window.'

" 'You and your budget,' I said, 'You are just like your mother.'

" 'My mother has nothing to do with this,' said Sally, and she walked away with the basket."

Larry felt a restraint on his liberty. He was being hemmed in by budgets and an inflexible wife. While this incident in itself might not be serious to a marriage, it was among others where the gist of the complaint was the assumption of command by one partner and the feeling of the other partner of being restrained and not knowing what to do about it.

Establishing a system of government is not easy. When Larry discussed the supermarket shopping adventure with me, we tried to place the incident as an historical event in the setting up of the rules of government in his newly formed family. When he originally came into the office, he felt as though he were fighting for his freedom. "I don't want to be married," he said. "I want to be like the other fellows. I want my freedom. I'm always being told what to do, what we can have, what we cannot have, what we can afford and what we cannot afford. I'm married to a boss."

We talked about Sally, his wife, and how she had learned early in her adolescence to care for herself and make her own way in spite of the objections of her parents. (Sally's parents objected to the wedding and did not attend.) Sally brought this independence into her marriage. She was determined to make ends meet and make a good marriage. She planned all household budgets carefully. She expected her husband to go along with her, since she went to the trouble of, and took the responsibility for, making the shopping lists and planning the menus.

Larry's placing the cookies into the basket without first discussing it with her took her by surprise, and instinctively she began defending herself—she had learned to jump to her own defense quickly. Because each bride and groom brings into a new marriage attitudes toward family living learned in his or her own family, they don't really know where and when their learned ways of behaving will conflict, until they begin to live as husband and wife.

In our interview Larry said, "I just thought it would be nice to have those cookies. Why can't a budget be flexible enough to allow for an unplanned purchase?"

"Why not? Have you offered to help with the budget?" I asked during our interview.

"No, I haven't," Larry said. "I thought if she wanted me to help, she would ask me."

As the conversation progressed, it soon became clear to Larry that his silence in the economic sphere at the beginning of their married life would have led Sally to believe that this was to be her responsibility and her decision. This is a well-established pattern in many families—the wife is given the job of family treasurer. This might have been the way economics was handled in Sally's family. However, in Larry's family, Larry's father and mother made many joint decisions about household expenditures of all kinds.

Larry now recognized that he had the responsibility

to tell Sally that he wanted the kind of family where the husband participates in making the budget and doing the shopping, and that he would have to take more affirmative steps to set up the kind of family system he wanted, instead of waiting for his wife to assume the initiative and then showing disappointment at her action.

From Sally's point of view, she saw a need—the need to budget—and she assumed the responsibility for it. She was expecting to be praised, perhaps, for assuming the obligation of budgeting. Yet, instead of praise for concern over the family finances, she was reprimanded by her husband for presuming to tell him that he could not put the cookies in the marketing basket.

From Larry's point of view the shopping episode changed from a joint experience in food purchasing to an encounter with his wife over his right to buy a box of cookies if he wanted to. Her putting the box back was the demonstration of an act of power. She was acting by authority of the budget which she herself had established.

Larry's placing of the box of cookies in the basket without first asking "the director of the budget" whether the budget allowed this purchase was, from her point of view, a disregard of all the work that went into making the budget, and the assumption of a right to make a purchase disregarding the budget. In a sense, from her point of view, Larry was asserting his power over her. So what began as a pleasant journey to the supermarket, an experience which could have been an enjoyable episode of doing things together, became a full-blown competition for power, including a slur upon Sally's mother.

Could This Competition Have Been Avoided?

Both Sally and Larry were acting upon assumed premises—that each would understand the other. In a new marriage assumptions of "correct ways" of interacting can be a source of friction. What is correct for one family is incorrect for another. Making judgments about "correct" and "incorrect" is often a source of trouble in itself. Some things may be acceptable under certain conditions, but not acceptable under others. Therefore, what I recommended is as follows:

When Larry placed the cookies in the box without asking Sally she, instead of instinctively replacing the cookies on the shelf, should have made an attempt to discuss the purchase with Larry. Of course, we can say, but Larry could have asked her if it was all right to put the cookies in the basket. That is also true. But not until Larry puts the cookies in the basket does this specific difference begin.

We must start with the point of interaction in order to look at what appears to be conflict. The conflict became visible when Sally put the cookies back. The moment she picked up the cookies there was a confrontation and a meeting of two wills. Since she didn't expect Larry to do the marketing, she could have clarified his act in this way: "Do you know this shopping list is very carefully budgeted and that cookies are not on the list?"

Larry would at that point have an opportunity either to abide by the budget or signal his desire to bypass the budget. If he chose not to abide by the budget, Sally would have to deal with other items on the list and perhaps juggle some other purchases, or they could have stopped for a moment, looked at the list, and decided together to substitute the cookies for some other item.

This could have been the beginning of a pattern for the new family—consultation on the shopping list before going to the supermarket. Or Sally might have learned something about Larry, i.e., the supermarket is no place to solve family problems. She might have learned that he is an impulse buyer and that before they go shopping they should agree on how to handle the urge for impulse buying. Depending upon what took place, perhaps Larry could learn from this experience that when Sally makes up a list, the list is made, and that unless he adds his input before the list is made, he had better leave the list alone once they get to the supermarket.

ALL OF THE ABOVE ASSUMES THE PARTNERS DO NOT ENJOY DIS-AGREEMENTS AND ARE TRYING TO BUILD A MUTUALLY SATIS-FYING MARITAL RELATIONSHIP.

If conflict and difference arise, marriage partners want to have, within their system of government, ways mutually agreed upon for taking account of conflict.

Morning and Night Persons

What happens when a *morning person* is married to a *night person*? Some marriages can survive this difference, others cannot. Ernest was a morning person and his wife, Stella, was a night person. Ernest went to bed at 9:30 P.M. Stella went to bed at 1:00 A.M. Ernest got up in the morning at the crack of dawn, bounced out of bed, went into the bathroom and turned on the water, turned on the radio, sang in the shower, got the kids up, gave them their breakfast, and got them off to school. Sometimes Stella got up before the children left to wave good-bye, but not always.

It wasn't always this way.

Stella came to the marriage counselor complaining about their sex life, saying Ernest was always asleep when she got into bed. She said it was impossible for her to go to bed before one in the morning. She had tried it, and she just tossed and turned and was miserable and prevented Ernest from sleeping. She said she wasn't even lovable when she went to bed early. She felt her husband should try to adjust his life to hers because he had more control over himself than she had over herself. Furthermore, nobody liked her in the morning when she got up to give the children breakfast. She was cross if the children made loud noises. She said nobody was to talk to her before she had her coffee. She answered no questions when they were asked. So why should she get up in the morning and get in everyone's way?

Ernest and Stella sat down to discuss their family problems, and they decided that they would respect Stella's "night person" needs by not asking her to get up in the morning to give the children breakfast. Stella's sexual needs and her attitudes about making known her sexual wishes became her responsibility. Stella had wanted to be sexually pursued, an attitude she had acquired growing up female. With a little sex education and some literature on adult sex, Stella agreed to try to initiate the sexual act. This pleased Ernest very much. He said he would never object to being awakened for sex.

Loner and Life-of-the-Party Persons

Have you ever observed a "loner–life-of-the-party" couple at a party? The loner goes off to a corner and reads the newspaper, or a book, or goes to sleep. The life of the party laughs, enjoys, mixes well, and when it is time to go home carefully nudges the loner and says, "Time to go home." This is a couple who have learned to live with their fundamental differences. The party person accepts the loner's wish to be left alone. Very often, the home climate of such a couple was stormy before they achieved this degree of harmony. It takes a good deal of maturity not to feel responsible for the so-called antisocial attitudes of a spouse. On the other hand, the loner spouse, who would rather not go to the party, goes to please the party-goer. From this point of view, just going is a social act. The life-of-the-party spouse learns not to feel responsible for the loner's behavior. Each person is his own keeper. Too many husbands and wives with this difference try to change the behavior of the loner, almost always unsuccessfully.

Learning to accept the difference and incorporating it into the expectation system of the family allows the family to continue to operate as a system.

Freedom and Flexibility

The marriage contract is different from all other contracts, because the political state becomes the automatic third party. But the state does not interfere until the parties try to dissolve the marriage or carry on in such a way that the children in the family call on the state as a substitute parent. We will discuss this further in the chapter on kinship, Chapter Five.

Unlike the other contractual relationships, American marriages are based on romantic love, with its psychological and emotional climate. Thus it is not possible for a contract to fit the two partners until they learn to know each other as husband and wife.

There are some limits, however, imposed by the political state. A wife and husband can promise each other that if for some reason they should fall out of love, they will give each other their freedom. Such a contract cannot be enforced because it is against public policy to permit the parties in marriage to agree on a dissolution. The state sets the conditions for dissolution. Some societies do permit such contracts and will enforce them. If one studies these societies, they will find a kinship different from our own. As I mentioned in Chapter One, the political system, economic system, and kinship system must be looked at as one comprehensive social network if we are to understand the limits placed upon the right to contract the terms of a marriage.

English common law, which is also American common law, and the law which governs the family in most states, says a married man must provide for the support of his wife and children. A husband and wife may contract that the wife should support the husband and she may do so. But what happens if the wife changes her mind during the marriage and wants her husband to support her? The law as it exists today in most states will enforce her right to support. Some people feel the passage of the Equal Rights Amendment will do away with the support obligation under common law. I disagree. Support is part of family law. The Equal Rights Amendment is personal law, applying to biological males and females. "Husband" and "wife" are status categories in family life and family law. If the rights and obligations of husband and wife are to be equal, then new family laws are needed along with the Equal Rights Amendment.

When the law gives two persons a license to wed, it says in effect that the state of being married is different from the state of being single. The rights and obligations are never spelled out; we are presumed to know them. These legal obligations do not become important in a marriage until the marriage begins to come apart.

How does the newly married couple learn what their family system is? Consider the following problem as it was discussed in a counseling interview with a married couple.

SHE: I thought it was the duty of the man to support his wife.

HE: Yes, but I thought marriage was a fifty-fifty proposition. I think we should pool our earnings and pay our expenses jointly, and save together.

SHE: I don't think so. After all, we do plan to have

children. I won't be able to work. I need to have some money of my own, to use without feeling I have to account to you.

HE: You feel the money in the joint savings account is not yours?

SHE: Well, I know my husband. He feels differently about money than I do. He calls me extravagant. I am not extravagant. Once in a while I do need something new, it makes me feel good. He feels clothes should be bought when you need something to wear. I don't want to have to fight with him and argue over these things. If I were allowed to keep my money now, we could live on his salary, adjust our standard of living to his income, and then when the baby comes we will know how to live on one salary. I think it is wrong to depend on the wife's salary. We don't plan for it always to be there.

HE: Well, I guess I am upset because I did expect that we were going into this marriage fifty-fifty.

ME: Fifty-fifty is a popular phrase, and it is pretty general. Let's try to find out exactly what fifty-fifty means to each of you.

To some couples, visiting the wife's parents once a year is equal to visiting the husband's every Sunday. The equal sign in marriage can mean something different to each married pair. It is important that there be a meeting of the minds about what is and what is not equal, and both agree upon the standards. Each partner must asume 100 percent responsibility for the marriage. Not every task can be divided fifty-fifty, nor should it be, if the family is to operate as an efficient and rewarding organization. In other words, each married pair creates a new political unit which provides for the use of power by each, according to a division of labor. Without some kind of order, one can predict anarchy and family instability.

But simply doing what the "law" of this tiny political entity requires does not make for a happy family. As each family discovers its own needs, it must have a way of evaluating whether its present "laws" are adequate. In the large political state, if laws fail to serve the people, the legislature is asked to pass new laws, or the courts are asked to reinterpret the law in the light of the society's life-styles. Every family, too, has these problems of legislation and adjudication. The family also has administrative functions similar to those of a governor. All of these functions—legislative, executive, and judicial—must be distributed between the husband and the wife. For instance, who determines when the family goes on vacation? Who decides whether the budget allows for savings? If the husband dislikes large parties and the wife loves them, who decides what kind of parties to give? Planning for such functions is sometimes possible, and is preferable to learning after confrontation.

Sometimes I ask young people coming to me for the first time to list the disappointments they have suffered since they were wed. This approach is especially helpful for people who find it difficult to verbalize their problems. It gives them the chance to put their complaints in writing.

Here is the report of a young man, age thirty-two, working days and going to school evenings. His wife was not working. They were living with his wife's mother. He wrote "what I expect" and "what I get."

"What I expect: I expect our home (even if 'our home'

is just one room in my mother-in-law's house) to be maintained in a reasonable degree of cleanliness and neatness. This means floor swept, furniture dusted, bureaus and desk straightened, clothes picked up and stored away (within space limits) and beds made up.

"What I get: Clothes are piled five and six deep on every available chair and in all four corners of the room. Summer and winter clothes are both stored in one small closet, thus limiting the room we need to hang up the clothes we are currently using. There is a thick coat of dust over every bit of furniture, except where my mother-in-law vacuums (approximately once every two weeks). Three or four sets of shoes are strewn about the floor, ignoring shoe bag which is hanging in the closet. Bureau tops are covered with bottles, hairpins, used Kleenex, clothes, and spilled powder. My desk is usually disarranged and clothes are piled on either end. Occasionally beds are not made."

At the top of the page he wrote a quotation from his wife: "A neat home is the sign of a compulsive neurotic."

His second page quotes his wife: "What shall I buy for your breakfast, dear—hot or cold cereal?"

"What I expect: I expect my wife to get up in the morning when I do and at least make breakfast for me. I have neither the time nor the talent for it. I do not consider this an exorbitant demand, since she does not have to make any lunches for me during the week, and I do not eat dinner at home four nights out of seven.

"What I get: I get my own breakfast every morning except on Sunday. Since I do not know how to cook, my breakfasts are limited to cold cereal or soft-boiled eggs.

This can get monotonous. I realize that I could learn to cook other things, but (a) I have very little free time because of night school, and (b) I'll be damned if I'll use my time to learn to do something I feel Alice should be doing. As a rule the kitchen sink is stocked with dirty supper dishes (my mother-in-law works nights till 11:30) and the general condition of the kitchen is so filthy I lose any enthusiasm for breakfast and wind up having coffee and a greasy doughnut at work at 8 A.M."

The title on the next page is, "Togetherness is for the birds!"

"What I expect: I expect my wife to recognize the fact that the 'bonds of matrimony' are intangible ones and stem rather from a moral responsibility and an emotional desire to share one's life. I fail to see why I should be forced to cater to the *neurotic* whim of an emotionally disturbed child who has a dread fear of being left alone. We are both individuals and although husband and wife, we have our own identities as to taste, values, philosophies of pleasure. After school is over, I intend to indulge in certain hobbies, specifically guns and hunting, which may exclude Alice, since she choses to dislike them and professes no interest in them. I realize that Alice is not an athletic person, but very much more of an intellectual than I. I want to see her enjoy herself with her own tastes and pleasures and mingle with the people who share her liking for poetry, art, writing, and classical music.

"I resent being called upon to act as chauffeur, bill-payer, and duenna, just so she can go to these intellectual hangouts and still enjoy the protected status of a married woman, particularly when these chores cause me to neglect my school work, which as I've told you is pretty important to me right now.

"What I get: I must account for every minute spent in some legitimate fashion, specifically work or school. Alice violently resents anything which might keep me from her. If I am fifteen minutes late coming home from school, she goes into a nagging harangue about a husband's duties to his wife. Along with this nagging is usually an accusation that I'm seeing some woman on the side. Any time I stop for a drink on the way home from school (two beers—fifteen minutes) I'm greeted at the door with the 'Inquisition' which starts before I even have time to take off my coat. If I should point out the fact that I was drinking with *men only,* then I'm accused of being homosexual and preferring their company to hers. In fact, anything or anyone who keeps me away from her side is a sign that I prefer them to her. The sight of me sitting down to read or watch television seems to enrage her, and although I know this isn't true, it seems as though she thinks up excuses to disturb me. Up until six months ago, I practically pleaded with her to find some interest of her own. Now since she has started writing poetry again and spending four or five nights a week in the Village, I guess I should have quit while I was ahead!"

This young man vividly describes married life from his point of view. Only the wife could tell her own point of view. But the husband did describe his wife's behavior as he saw it and his discontent with it.

In this relationship, there was chaos. Husband and wife could not agree on housekeeping procedures, meal preparation, laundry and cleanliness, the right to some private time, financial programs, and responsibility and attitudes toward each other's friends. Each was frozen into a particular philosophy of what was right, and therefore there was no room for any other point of view. It is interesting to note what is important to this man.

Take breakfast, for example. In some families, breakfast is not a marital issue at all. In others, breakfast is a serious issue. Over the years I have seen women, who had never wanted to get up for breakfast with their husbands, discover that by getting up they enhanced their relationship—they learned more about their husbands at the breakfast table than at any other time.

On the other hand, some men who had insisted that their wives get up to make breakfast have learned that their wives cannot be civil in the morning and that bad temper and morning arguments are even less desirable than not getting breakfast at home.

To some people who read this, the question of breakfast may seem trivial. Yet in my interviews with unhappily married people, a husband will frequently say, "And she never once got up to make me my breakfast!" I have asked one or two of these men, "Have you ever told your wife how much it means to you to have your breakfast at home?" The answer has been, "No, she should *know* this. I won't ask her."

This feeling that the wife should have known—isn't it the duty of the wife to make breakfast for her husband?—interferes with the husband's attitudes toward asking. He assumes that because the wife doesn't, she doesn't want to, and making assumptions, without checking, can become a marital sore spot, as in this instance.

Breakfast for many partners is a symbol of one person's caring for the other. Another common symbol of caring is the demonstration of affection, like the kiss. If the wife expects her husband to kiss her when he leaves for work, then she must either tell him to kiss her, ask him to kiss her, or kiss him to show by example what she would like. How is the husband to know that a kiss is expected of him? The wife who says her husband should know he should kiss her has expectations based upon her own assumptions. She interprets the husband's failure to perform these acts as willful and hostile. Most married people do not know that all of these assumptions are learned in their childhood. So, if you want a kissing husband, or a breakfast-making wife, you must help your spouse to be one.

How does romantic love fit into a cold and calculating approach to marriage? A "system of family government" certainly doesn't sound very romantic.

Family government depends upon respect and love. In countries that prefer arranged marriages, young people enter into marriage with respect for the decision of their parents. This respect takes them over the hurdles of adjustment to marriage. It is the hope of these parents that their children when married will learn to love each other. I know husbands and wives in arranged marriages. They too love each other in the same way as couples in nonarranged marriages.

In the United States romantic love carries the bride and groom over the hurdles of getting settled into the routines of marriage. Unlike arranged marriages, which begin with respect, our marriages develop respect from romantic love. After and along with respect develops what I like to call "married love." Married love comes after a slow process of ironing out a system of mutual expectations with latitude for error and "nonaccountability" for mistakes built into the system. "Nagging" is one expression of accountability—the right to know, the assumption of power asserted by one partner over the other. Inquisition or cross-examination is a familiar complaint. Nagging is a sign of competition for power, evidence of lack of mutuality in the family system.

I remember the case of a West Indian woman who was accused of being a nag by her husband. She said her husband's job ended at 4:30 in the afternoon, yet he never got home until 6 P.M. for dinner. She had no objection to six o'clock as the dinner hour. Her objection was that her husband wouldn't tell her where he had been, and she felt she had a right to know. Where did this "right to know" come from, I asked. She said, "It's the law. Every American wife has the right to know where her husband is from the time he leaves work until he gets home." Although recently arrived from the West Indies, she was now American and wanted to live American-style.

A common marital problem reported by men centers around the "dinner nag," while a common complaint from the wife concerns the husband who promises to be home for dinner, doesn't come until much later, and doesn't call. When he gets home he expects his wife to be glad to see him. Instead, what he gets is, "I have been knocking my head against the wall. Why didn't you call? You can eat your cold dinner all by yourself. I am going to bed!" The disappointed husband says, "She only cares about her dinner. She doesn't care what happens to me."

Not all late husbands get this kind of treatment. A husband who says he will be home for dinner may not be expected to arrive on time by the experienced wife, who has learned that her husband cannot be on time. She therefore does not get angry when he comes late. She may find herself still expecting him but trying to handle her own disappointment. If it is obvious to her that her husband is not going to change, will she learn to accept it? She should ask herself, "What are my alternatives?" Perhaps she will discover that she can either enjoy her husband *whenever* he comes, or be hostile. Either of these attitudes toward being late can become part of the family system. Many men who come home late habitually, and whose wives habitually nag, learn to accept the "nagging wife." Some even say, "She has a right to nag." The latitude is as flexible as the partners' personalities will permit. Thus, what might be absolutely impossible behavior in one marriage, might be acceptable in another. Conflict in and of itself does not cause a marriage to disintegrate.

Most families learn through conflict and argument the dos and don'ts of their political systems. Few, if any, families start with deliberately defined rules for making decisions, and the search for some order chips away at the stability of the new marriage. But knowing that some kind of political system is "built in" in every marriage should help the partners to change from "hit and miss" political decision-making, with its disappointments, to a more systematic distribution of executive, legislative, and judicial rights and obligations between the marriage partners.

The Written Contract As PreMarriage Work

When marriage partners ask me: "If we had made a written marriage contract, would we have been spared the conflicts, misunderstandings, and quarrels that brought us to a marriage counselor?" I tell them:

Written marriage contracts do attempt to fill out some of the uncertainties of the unwritten contract. Of course, a young couple about to be married who think of marriage as a mini-government, a mini-business, and a mini-society will have much more to talk about and decide before marriage than a couple who at random, off-the-cuff, try to provide for the uncertainties of marriage.

The making of a written marriage contract is an opportunity for the about-to-be-married (and the already married, too) to take a careful look at the marriages around them and discuss what they would like for themselves and what they would not like. Also, the writing itself is an experience and a model for the future exchange of ideas, feelings, differences, and agreements.

If the partners to the written contract look upon it as an aid to helping them to be better informed married partners and as a reference for future use in case of disagreement, then a written contract can only be an asset in the marriage. *But,* if the partners look upon the contract as a legal document to be enforced according to the letter, with no flexibility to correct for misjudgments and mistakes, then a written marriage contract will probably have as many pitfalls for a good marriage as does the traditional unwritten one.

For instance, delegating tasks can minimize conflict. However, task contracts by themselves are no guarantee of a good marriage. Why not? Because most agreements are made in good faith, but marriage is so complicated that the unforeseen is all but inevitable. Some task and agreement conditions which ideally should have been made in advance are simply unknown at the time of the initial contractual agreement.

IT TAKES A GOOD DEAL OF SHARING TO KNOW WHAT SHOULD GO INTO AN IDEAL MARRIAGE CONTRACT.

For example, I remember the case of a young couple who had been married for twelve years and who had two children, ages nine and ten. Before their marriage, the husband, a Baptist, promised his wife and a Catholic priest that the children would be raised as Catholics. Religious difference was no problem at the time of the marriage and while the children were little. However, when the children became old enough to ask questions such as, "Why don't you come to church with us, Dad?" the husband's latent attitudes about church began to appear. He became aware that he wanted to share a religious experience with his children. He did not renege on his agreement to have the children raised as Catholics, but he wanted them to share his experience at his church, too. He asked his wife to let the children go to church with him on Sunday. But his wife's definition of being "raised Catholic" did not permit the children to go to another church.

In the above case, the full impact of the contract's meaning, the emotional overtones of the father-child sharing experience, was not considered at the time of the marriage. And the contract made no provision for change.

A GOOD MARRIAGE CONTRACT PROVIDES NOT ONLY FOR WHAT EACH PARTNER MUST DO, BUT ALSO FOR ADJUSTMENTS IF, FOR SOME UNFORESEEN REASON, THE CONTRACT CANNOT BE FUL-FILLED.

It is worthy of repetition to say: Written contracts are good when the partners use them as counseling aids, and not legal documents; when the contracts seek stability, not rigidity; and when the contracts express a willingness to respect those differences that were not predictable and became known during the marriage.

Four

§

Marriage Is
an Economic System

After the wedding the business of marriage
begins and not all lovers are
good business partners immediately.

Every married couple is in business—the business of family living. If the goal of commercial business is to increase profit, the goal of family living is to increase domestic tranquillity and personal happiness. Marriage partners are expected to negotiate and trade the commodities of money, time, love, affection, trust, respect, loyalty, and even compassion for the services necessary to keep the family functioning for the good of all.

Every family needs a body of rules for the management of household affairs, observed Aristotle in his treatise *Oikonomica,* so he invented the science of economics, which means "the management of household affairs." But by some quirk of history the study of economics became the foundation of business, and husbands and wives were left to work out or fight out the economics of family life.

"Exchange," a key concept in business, is equally central in marriage. The wedding knot literally ties husband and wife into a web of reciprocal services, and no member of the family is immune. Even the infant exchanges love and trust for supportive services.

"Negotiation," another business concept, is as important to spouses as it is to business partners. Domestic bankruptcy is an economic disaster.

In English common law, before women were legal persons, wives were in an unfair economic bind within the family. They couldn't own property in their own names, and they couldn't work outside the family without the consent of their husbands. When they did, their pay belonged to the husband. Bad as conditions were, husbands and wives were never obligated to each other as employer-employee.

Even though some feminists feel that wives would be better off if their husbands were required by law to pay them a salary, making the husband-wife kinship purely economic would be degrading to women. Granted that wives, as partners, in many marriages have not shared in the prosperity of their husbands, the solution is not to change the relationship from partners to employer-employee.

The solution is better education for marriage, more information about what a good marriage can be, and public support for the difficult task of establishing a good marriage. Husbands and wives must establish through negotiation and trade their own special economic system.

THERE ARE AS MANY WAYS FOR COUPLES TO SHARE IN THE GIVING AND TAKING OF THE ECONOMIC SYSTEM AS THERE ARE MARRIED COUPLES. EACH COUPLE IS UNIQUE.

Some couples insist on separate careers, separate financial records, and all household tasks by contract. Other couples, like President and Mrs. Carter and President and Mrs. Reagan, see the husband's career as a joint effort with a division of labor between them that enhances their lives as partners. Whichever way the partners choose, all partners in marriage are in an economic enterprise and must address needs, wants, the distribution of goods and services, and fiscal responsibility.

Most men and women go into marriage as an affair of the heart, with little or no planning for the large number of business decisions that need immediate attention in the change from single personhood to partnership.

Every family needs a fiscal policy. Very few married people come to marriage with well-thought-out fiscal policies. A few do come without any thought about money and their future. Disagreements come quickly when the partners see how much they differ on how to deal with money, time, and services. Learning to balance between a too tightly planned household, rigid and inflexible, and a too loosely planned household, upset with chaos, is marriage work.

Mr. and Mrs. Robert M. Takem

Mr. and Mrs. Takem are great in bed together; their trouble is in the checkbook.

"If my wife cares so little about me and the terrible financial bind I'm in that she won't sell the summer cottage," said Mr. Takem, "then I don't care to live with her. She can have that place in Wisconsin; I hate it. I hate the weekend trip. I hate being home in Chicago alone all week, I hate spending my weekend fixing the bikes, screens, and everything else the kids break during the week. Next week they are broken again."

Mr. Takem jumped out of his chair and began to walk in small circles. In a slow, deliberate voice, we heard, "That is what I mean. She tells me I love it when I just said I hate that place. Sure, I like my boat when I am on it, but I want to give that up too. It costs too much money."

This is spring 1974 and Mr. Takem's stocks, like almost everyone's, have taken a licking in the market. Mr. Takem's income comes from the selling of technological instruments, and for the moment the cash flow doesn't warrant the plans for expansion to which he is committed. Mr. Takem worries whether he will have enough money to send the boys to college in two years, whether he will have enough to make the necessary house repairs.

When Mrs. Takem offers to move to a smaller house, she, at the same time, questions whether that would really save anything because she feels sure that if they move, Mr. Takem will want new furniture.

Mr. Takem hears the word furniture and begins his complaints about the lack of care for furniture. He goes on, "She doesn't care about money. Her car is full of old McDonald's wrappers and cups; the dogs chew the tables in the study; the children put wet glasses on the television."

"He wants everything we spend money on to remain in perfect condition," said Mrs. Takem.

"We are living beyond our means. The bank wants a down payment on that building I'm buying for my place of business and my wife won't sell that summer cottage and let me use the money for my business," Mr. Takem said angrily.

There was a history to the purchase of the summer cottage. Originally the Takems had rented the cottage. When it came on the market Mrs. Takem said that if Mr. Takem would buy it, she promised that if ever he needed the money, she would sell it.

"I think the cottage is a good investment," said Mrs. Takem. "It will be worth more later on. Why don't you borrow on your insurance?"

"And now she is trying to run my business." Mr. Takem was furious. Mrs. Takem would not run the household according to his instructions, and now she dared to tell him how to run his business!

After a moment of silence, he said, "And what if something should happen to me? Then what would you say if the insurance money wasn't available for you and the kids?"

Mr. and Mrs. Takem had come to see the marriage counselor specifically to resolve the impasse created when Mr. Takem asked Mrs. Takem for the house, according to their agreement. Mrs. Takem admitted she had made the agreement, but felt Mr. Takem hadn't demonstrated to her that he needed to sell the house. She felt instead that he needed to be sure he was in control. She said, "He resents that I enjoy my summers so much."

Mr. Takem denied he resented Mrs. Takem's enjoyment of the summer house. He just disliked the great inconvenience it created for him. "But," he said, "enjoyment is not the issue. I need the money. The cottage is in her name and I want her to sell it."

Mr. Takem, when he agreed to come to a marriage counselor, thought, in his own mind, that the counselor would prevail upon Mrs. Takem to abide by her promise to sell the summer cottage.

Mrs. Takem, when she suggested going to a marriage counselor, wanted to find a place where she could say what was on her mind because she found she could never have a conversation at home with her husband on a subject about which he felt strongly. She said, "He talks me down. I just stop talking."

We agreed that Mrs. Takem would get a chance to tell her story without interruption by Mr. Takem. Twice, Mr. Takem started to interrupt. Each time Mrs. Takem said, "I know what you are going to say. I have heard it all before."

It was a very surprised Mr. Takem who heard, "I always know what you are going to say, you have said it so many times before, but you wouldn't like it if I kept interrupting you!"

Mrs. Takem went on to say what the summer house meant to her—a summer freedom. She reluctantly admitted to her promise to sell, and said she would abide by her promise if she were sure the need really did exist. She had to be sure this demand was not Mr. Takem's way of punishing her for spending "too much money for the children's clothing," for failing to live up to Mr. Takem's standards of cleanliness and order in the home and in her car, and for failing somehow to be responsible for what the children did that annoyed Mr. Takem.

"I wish my husband could learn to relax just a little," said Mrs. Takem.

"Relax?" asked Mr. Takem. "How can I relax when I need the money for the bank and the only place I know where that money can come from is the sale of the cottage. You don't trust my business judgment."

Mrs. Takem volunteered that she was proud of her husband. He started as a salesman for someone else and now owned his own very successful business. Furthermore, she loves her husband and wants to stay married to him.

"Kate," Mr. Takem said, "believe me, I wouldn't be asking you to give up the cottage if I didn't think it was absolutely necessary in order to meet the loan."

Without enthusiasm for what she was about to say, Mrs. Takem said, "The cottage is yours if that is the only way.out."

Mr. Takem was not happy with her answer. "You don't think you should give it up?"

"I don't know if I will be fit to live with," said Mrs. Takem. Mrs. Takem stopped short.

"Is there something else you would like to say?" I asked Mrs. Takem.

"I thought my husband should at least say, 'Thank you, I'll make it up to you,'" she said.

"I cannot take the cottage if you feel that way," said Mr. Takem.

"But we all depend upon your business," said Mrs. Takem, "and if in your judgment it is necessary, I guess it must be."

The Takems agreed to negotiate a listening contract at home to discuss their feelings about the summer cottage. At the next meeting, which took place three weeks later, only because Mr. Takem was not able to come sooner, Mrs.

Takem reported that they had been able to have a long discussion about the cottage and it wasn't as important to her as it had seemed. This time she told Mr. Takem she would sell the cottage with a voice that sounded like she wanted to sell it.

Mrs. Takem had some other matters she wanted to discuss. Was it necessary for Mr. Takem to be so concerned about the condition of her car, the condition of the furniture, which he called *his* furniture, and other household matters?

"Does the condition of Mrs. Takem's car bother you?" I asked Mr. Takem. "Does it bother you enough to make you want to do something about cleaning it up?"

"Yes, it does," said Mr. Takem. "If she cannot take it in to be washed, I will do it."

Mrs. Takem decided she could not promise when her car could be released for washing. "But if he will pay for the wash job, and not take it out of my allowance, I will have it washed every week," she said.

Also, Mrs. Takem said she could not control the children to the extent that Mr. Takem demanded of her. Couldn't he establish his own relationship with the children about *his* furniture?

I suggested that perhaps Mr. Takem should see if he could think about "family furniture" and "his furniture."

Mrs. Takem said she did not enjoy Mr. Takem's need to dominate "how the house works." Couldn't she be in charge of the house and he the business? she proposed to Mr. Takem. Mr. Takem promised to think about that proposition. He thought he was being nice to his wife by suggesting ways of running a more efficient house.

Two weeks later the Takems returned.

They reported they were using the listening contract with greater ease. Mr. Takem had changed his mind about selling the summer cottage. He had found another way to meet the bank down payment.

But he had one problem to discuss today—gifts. Mrs. Takem was going to have a birthday in a few days. Mr. Takem had stopped giving her gifts and he wanted to talk about it in the counselor's office.

"When I give my wife a gift," he said, "I expect her to keep it."

Mrs. Takem said she felt it was the right of the recipient to return or keep a gift. Sometimes she felt that the money spent for the gift item could be better used for something else she wanted.

Mr. Takem was personally offended by the return of a gift he had chosen. He prided himself on his taste. And Mrs. Takem agreed he had very good taste. He saw the gift as a giving of part of himself. Mrs. Takem saw the gift and weighed it on the scale of "Was it worth the money and could I buy something else with it?"

Mr. Takem said, "If you want something else, buy it yourself."

But Mrs. Takem liked receiving a present. Now that she was told what the rules would be, could she learn to accept the conditions under which her husband would resume the practice?

"In a house where money is so important," said Mrs. Takem, "I guess I can learn there is more to a gift than whether it is the best use of the money."

What can the do-it-yourself marriage counselor learn from the case of Mr. and Mrs. Takem?

Did the Takems live happily ever after? They lived

more happily than before they came to counseling. The Takems learned that each one is responsible for his or her own happiness. For example, Mr. Takem's complaints about the condition of Mrs. Takem's car could be diminished if he did something about getting the car cleaned up.

The Takem case describes a not atypical family. Mr. and Mrs. Takem do not agree on how to manage the affairs of the Takem family. They must decide if there is room for more than one point of view on how the family should operate. Sometimes a husband, who is chief executive in his business, brings his "executive personality" home without realizing a family chooses its own executives and he might not be the chief at home. Mr. Takem's "executive personality" was interfering with Mrs. Takem's concept of her executive role in the family.

The case history shows the Takems in the process of dealing with their differences. They both discovered that differences cannot be ignored. When Mrs. Takem disregarded Mr. Takem's statement of dislike for the summer cottage and said, "You like it," she lost an opportunity to discuss their differences. When the family is seen as a business, differences are negotiable.

Mr. and Mrs. Walters

This couple came for counseling to find out why they weren't getting along better, since they both felt they had so much going for them—all of the benefits of suburban living, including good children, a nice home, no particular financial problems, and not disliking each other.

The Walters have been married for fifteen years and have four children, two younger girls and two older boys, ages five to thirteen. Mr. Walters feels that he is a good husband and father and doesn't know why, as he says, "things aren't better between us."

Mrs. Walters states what I call the lament of the suburban mother. "Yes, he provides well for his family; we have plenty to eat. But he is never home. He never spends any time with us. He doesn't show us that he loves us."

Hardly had Mrs. Walter finished her last two words, when her husband shouted, "You complain that I work every night. For whom do you think I am working? For myself? You like nice things, you want a pretty house, you want the children to play hockey, take ice skating lessons, go to summer camp for two months, and do everything all the other children in the neighborhood do. Well, I want the same things for them and I am doing it the only way I know how—by working my tail off!" At the end of the sentence he found himself at the very edge of his chair, leaning forward and pointing his finger at his wife. Silently, he relaxed, let his head fall and said nothing more.

Mrs. Walters kept looking at him, and after a minute, she very slowly, as if measuring each word to avoid ambiguity, began, "I don't think you *have* to work every night; you could learn to make better use of your time."

"What's the use of coming here? I give up! She *always* knows what *I* should do. Sometimes I think I ought to let her go out and see how hard it is to earn the dollar," he said quietly. The air in the room was filled with his feeling of disappointment. He had expected his wife to acknowledge his sacrifice and affection for his family as documented by his long hours spent working. Instead his wife was judging the way he spent his time and told him he didn't spend it well. He didn't like being judged. Instead of being just angry, he said, "Here is proof that we just don't have what it takes to get along."

What Mr. Walters didn't say was, "I want my wife to tell me she appreciates how hard I work. She didn't even tell me 'You are doing a good job.'"

Mrs. Walters wanted more than time and money from her husband. She wanted an opportunity to tell her husband that she and the children needed him in another way. Her own needs prevented her from listening to her husband's plea of, "Please tell me something nice about what I am doing." She was interested in starting a conversation about her needs, leaving the prior conversation with Mr. Walters dangling.

I suggested that we begin the whole interview over again and that this time both would stay with one subject at a time.

Mr. Walters obligingly repeated what he had said earlier about how hard he worked for his children to give them the things their mother wanted for them. When he finished, I asked Mrs. Walters, "What idea did you hear?"

"That he is working so hard, not for himself, but for us."

"Now, what feelings did you hear?"

"He feels he is doing a great job and we should be pleased and happy about everything he is doing for us."

"That's right!" Mr. Walters responded brightly, "and please tell me I am a good provider."

"You are a good provider of money," his wife agreed,

"but there is more than money to life. We need to see more of you, we like you, we want you to enjoy some of our projects with us." She stopped, looked at me as though she was unsure about going forward. "How do I tell him now that I think he could use his time better?" she asked.

"That is a good question. Why don't you share your uncertainty with your husband? Tell him you need help to say something which might upset him, even though you don't intend to make him angry." I coached her as she tried to learn a new conversational skill.

She continued, "John, can you help me?"

"If it is more money," John said jokingly, "no."

"It's about your spending more time with us, and I have some ideas. Will you hear me out?"

"I'll listen, but I don't promise anything."

"O.K., just listen or even tell me what ideas you have."

Again I intervened to help Mrs. Walters use this time as a learning period to keep the ball of communication bouncing. "Please be as specific as you can with your recommendations. Is there one evening in the week you particularly would like your husband to come home? Or are you thinking of redoing the whole night work arrangement? Let us deal with one at a time."

Mr. Walters, to whom the night work was familiar complaint, intervened this time, saying, "I think I understand what my wife wants, she wants me to go to the skating rink with her and the boys on Tuesday nights because other fathers go. She thinks I don't love the boys because I don't do things with them. Maybe we should sit down at home and talk this all out. If my whole family would like me better if I didn't work one night a week, I should talk about it."

And the Walters did work out an exchange. For one night a week he received the affection from his sons and his wife which he needed.

Mrs. Walters thought the boys needed their father. She took his working as a lack of interest in their development. Her attitude was: If you are not interested in our boys I am not interested in you. She was jealous of the other women at the rink whose husbands either skated with their children or were there to help them with their skates and act as an audience.

Mr. Walters did go to the rink on Tuesday and he found himself helping the boys with their skates. Although he didn't skate, he began to talk to the other fathers about skating and became part of the Tuesday night group. The boys were delighted with this new attention from their father and his relationship with the other fathers. Mrs. Walters was pleased with her husband every time she heard the boys say how much better skating was since Dad came along. Mr. Walters was surprised to find how much he was enjoying the experience and how easy he found the time to give on Tuesday night. He told his wife he was unconsciously dragging his feet at work because things were not good at home. As all members of the Walters family exchanged time and affection, the climate of family cooperation improved.

Dr. and Mrs. Salutake

Dr. and Mrs. Salutake are living apart by agreement. They came to the marriage counselor to discuss certain conditions for the return of Mrs. Salutake to the family home.

Mrs. Salutake is forty-nine, but looks much younger, since her "down" facial lines were removed by surgery about two years ago. This isn't a part of her life history she tells everyone, and she was somewhat upset that her husband had mentioned it. But the doctor was trying to make a point about the way money is spent in their family, so she forgave him for telling her secret. Not that the doctor didn't approve of the face-lift: he did, and he adored his wife and her very good looks. However, as a precondition of her returning home, Mrs. Salutake was asking the doctor to guarantee her that he would pay for some mouth reconstruction she wanted to have done in the city where she was temporarily living.

When the Salutakes separated, she moved out of the small town where her husband practices general medicine. Prior to her moving, all of her dentistry was done in Balfour, where the doctor lives and where the dental and medical men exchange services to members of their respective families. In the city her new dentist advised Mrs. Salutake she would need periodontal work and caps on all of her teeth—to the tune of two thousand dollars.

Dr. Salutake listened, and when his wife finished he asked her to look at him, particularly his low-slung jaw. "It is a question of priorities," he said. "I know I need corrective mouth surgery, I have had a bad bite for many years, but we have two kids in college and one child in prep school and I thought I should wait until we could better afford it."

Suddenly he stopped talking. After a few moments of silence, he resumed, "I am trying to listen to myself. I don't want to attack you, as you so often say I do, or accuse you of lack of concern for our financial obligations. I don't know how to say what I want to say, without sounding nasty."

Mrs. Salutake's curiosity was aroused. "Just say it," she said.

"Well," the doctor went on, "why don't you come back to town and have my dentist look at your mouth?"

If Mrs. Salutake had not been forewarned that Dr. Salutake was aware that she would be displeased by what he had said, she might have been angrier than she was. "Your dentist is the one who got me into this mess," she said.

"All right, then we'll have a third dentist look at you, but the only reason you went to that dentist in Boston is because your cousin went to him and had all that work done and you want it, too!" said the doctor.

The conversation which had started out as a request for money by Mrs. Salutake to have mouth rehabilitation was becoming a personal criticism of Mrs. Salutake and her need to be more beautiful than her cousin.

"My wife is always in competition with her cousin. Did I tell you that her cousin had undergone facial surgery before she did?" he asked me, while looking at his wife.

Turning to Mrs. Salutake, I said, "Your husband wants to make sure that what your dentist is advising is absolutely necessary for you. How do you feel about that?"

The doctor and his wife then decided to ask the dentist how much was necessary and how much of the dental work he suggested was elective.

A few minutes later, Mrs. Salutake said she would re-

consider her request. "Would you just pay for the periodontal work and I will pay for the recapping of the teeth?"
she asked.

Mrs. Salutake had other financial matters to discuss,
she said, and wanted to change the subject.

Mrs. Salutake received a weekly allowance from the
doctor for food for the house and certain regular personal
needs like hairdressing. In addition, she had charge
accounts at all of the major stores in Boston. But she
wanted some "free" spending money—not earmarked for
any special purpose.

The doctor replied to her request with, "You have
access to the bank account. Take it."

"No, I want you to give it to me," said Mrs. Salutake.

"She won't use the bank account," the doctor said,
"and I don't know why."

Mrs. Salutake went on to explain that she felt uncomfortable using the bank account. "My mother used to get a
set sum every week for herself from my father," she said,
"and I would like that too."

The doctor agreed to discuss the amount of the sum
with her later.

"I have another item of family business," said Mrs.
Salutake. "I have never mentioned this to you before,"
she said, turning to the doctor. "On Friday, when I finish
at the beauty parlor, I feel like going out to dinner. But
you pick up Richard at school on Friday. The two of you
have dinner and then you take him to a hockey game or
baseball or football, and I am left alone. Sometimes I call
your father and take him out to dinner just to be with
someone."

"I thought you liked my taking Richard to sports," the doctor said. "Why didn't you say something sooner?"

"It sounded awful," she said, "like I was jealous."

The doctor invited Mrs. Salutake to go to the games with him and Richard. I felt, from the look on Mrs. Salutake's face, that this was not an ideal solution for her, but she evidently decided to accept the offer. She wanted the doctor's time on Friday night. She got his time with certain conditions attached for sharing it with her son at sports events.

During the several interviews with the Salutakes, the doctor raised the question of "looking in the other person's wallet" without first asking permission.

Mrs. Salutake said that on certain occasions she did go into the doctor's wallet and take some money. She felt it was not an unusual act, that many wives took money from their husband's wallets and that her mother had taken money from her father's wallet. But, she said, if she had her own "free" spending money she wouldn't need to go to the doctor's wallet. And, as an aside, she told the doctor she did not want him to go into her wallet!

I mention this wallet incident because sometimes children, when they become married adults, repeat the customs they observed in their families when growing up. In this case, Mrs. Salutake generalized her own childhood experience into an acceptable marital custom. But it was not acceptable to her husband. He said, in his family, his mother never took money from his father's wallet. He said he supported the idea of husbands and wives sharing the family monies, but felt a man's wallet was his private affair.

Since the Salutakes were renegotiating many financial agreements between them before the return of Mrs. Salutake to the family home, they agreed between themselves that wallets were to be private property.

You might ask, can renegotiated marriages be successful?

The Salutakes felt their spelling out of all of the differences between them concerning money and its uses would help them have a better marriage. They were very happy with their social life and sex life as husband and wife. But the money problem, although encountered early in their marriage, was never faced and discussed until Mrs. Salutake moved out of the family home temporarily and got a job in a nearby town.

Married women who do not work have no money except that given to them by their husbands. During a marriage, a wife has no legal right to share her husband's financial assets. The law assumes that the husband and wife will work it out. The law is very vague—something about a wife being entitled to support while she is living with her husband. Dr. Salutake was supporting his wife. But not in the style which she would have liked and which she thought the doctor's income warranted. He also had sex-stereotyped attitudes about "his" money, instead of the attitude of "our" money, a more acceptable point of view for "marriage as a partnership."

When a husband and wife separate, the legal presumption, that a husband and wife will work out their business relationship satisfactorily, disintegrates. Now the marriage partners begin to negotiate, usually with the intervention of lawyers. Lawyers look into the whole financial picture of the family and support must be related to the family income. In this case, during the separation, Mrs. Salutake was getting a certain sum of money each week for herself, agreed upon by the lawyers.

As a result of this experience, the doctor's attitude toward his role as the distributor of monies changed. Mrs. Salutake would have preferred that the change could have come about without her leaving. But she tried and was not successful. She preferred being married and was happy to renegotiate her return to the family home.

Why have I included in this book a case where the parties are living apart but preparing to live together again?

In my long experience, I have discovered that many married couples separate voluntarily during a marriage and then return to each other without renegotiating their marriages. The household breaks down and one or the other leaves out of frustration. Without renegotiation of household management there is no reason to expect that the breakdown will not be repeated.

Not all families need lawyers to help them renegotiate. If the partners can create the proper climate for communication, they can renegotiate their own marriages.

Money, Money, Money

THERE ARE NO APPROVED CUSTOMS FOR THE HANDLING OF MONEY MATTERS WITHIN A FAMILY.

"Every morning I tell my husband what I plan to do that day, what I intend to buy and where, and he estimates the amount of money I will need for that day," says Marie Upright, who says she likes this system because it keeps the accounts simple. John Doad, on the other hand, prefers his way. "I give my wife my total salary. We figure out how much I will need for lunch and carfare, and she gives that much back to me. I don't ask her what she does with the money. She takes care of everything."

So long as both partners agree on a procedure, money, and the handling of it, is not a family problem. But where there is no agreement, deficit spending, unbalanced budgets, and financial chaos can change a "being in love" to a "being out of love."

The increased availability of credit for consumer purchasing increases economic dissention. Let us listen to Richard, age twenty-four:

"I have explained my methods for trying to pay back bills to my wife. Every time I sit down to do this, I am subjected to sneers and ridicule for making a fuss over bills. My wife Alice has perfected what I call the 'Gypsy Approach to Financial Obligations.' She learned it from her mother. They both show the most callous indifference to anyone they owe money to. They sincerely think that people were put on this earth solely to serve them and they don't feel the slightest obligation to pay them, except at their own leisure."

Richard didn't object to the bills, just his wife's attitude toward his method of payment. My question to Richard was: "Could you learn to disregard your wife's snickers so long as you believe you are doing the right thing for you? You say the bills are your responsibility and you are willing to deal with them, while your wife's attitudes toward payment are hers with no responsibility. Is there anything you can do about your wife's attitudes?''

Of course Richard knew he could deal only with his own attitudes. He could tell his wife her attitudes didn't please him, if that would make him feel better, but there was no way he could change his wife's attitudes.

Both Richard and Alice believed in credit buying, their conflict was over payment for credit.

Some couples, however, differ over the philosophy of fiscal policy. Mrs. Ward was against "pretending." Her husband said his boss recommended that he trade in his beat-up Chevrolet for a new car. Against the wishes of Mrs. Ward, her husband purchased a new car on the installment plan. In addition, he began to charge gas whereas previously they had always paid cash. Bills began to mount and Mrs. Ward was worried. She would scream at bill collectors. Soon her husband began to lie about his purchases since every night she would ask, "What did you charge today?"

What could Mrs. Ward do? Mr. Ward did eventually pay the bills. She had to learn to disregard the bill collectors since the payment of bills was not within her control. Could she learn to say, "My husband is in charge of all finances, you will have to see him?" An alternative would be to find a suggestion for change that Mr. Ward could accept.

Can change be motivated by the partner who dislikes what is being done about household finances? Traditionally, married women, dependent upon their husbands for money, have tried to "fight fair," but when they find they are ineffective with words, they try the withdrawal of paticipation in sexual relations. So many of them have said to me, "What else can I do?"

Listen to Mrs. Arndt. Although her husband earned a very nice salary, he spent the major part of it on clothes for himself. He said it was necessary for his job. Mrs. Arndt felt the family lived well below the standard they should have been able to afford. In desperation she refused to prepare meals for her husband, encouraged the children to call him Mr. Tightwad, and refused to have sex with him. What happened to the marriage? It didn't improve. Mrs. Arndt came to see me because she wanted to stay married. What new alternatives were open to her, if any? Her goal was to keep this business of marriage solvent and find ways to encourage a better relationship between the partners.

Mr. Arndt was a businessman. He too wanted to keep his family life solvent and was willing to negotiate. The Arndts learned to talk about "what this family needs" instead of Mrs. Arndt complaining that her husband spent too much on himself.

The Remarried Family

Are the economic problems of the remarried family different from the economic problems of the first-married family?

All remarried families have the same household management problems as the first-marriage family, plus. When economic obligations to the previous marriage or marriages still exist, they become part of the economics of the remarriage. A divorce dissolves the bond of matrimony, but not the bond of economic responsibility for children.

Let me just note a problem or two that could arise in many remarried families. Perhaps these are problems in your marriage.

THE CHARLES FAMILY

Mrs. Charles has two children by her present husband. When Mr. Charles married her, he knew that her three children by a previous marriage were living with their father. A year after their marriage, the three children wrote to their mother and asked if they could come and live with her.

After reading the letter, given to him by his wife, Mr. Charles told his wife the children could not come to live with them. Mr. Charles worked as a maintenance man and they lived in a modest three bedroom house, just big enough for the present Charles family of four.

But the children came anyway, because their father had taken a job in a foreign country and they did not want to live with their grandparents.

Once there, room was found somehow for them to sleep, but Mr. Charles said he would not support them. Mrs. Charles applied for Aid to Families with Dependent Children and received financial help.

Mr. Charles asked his wife to turn over these funds to him. Mrs. Charles refused. She said she needed the money for clothing and extras like fees for the hockey rink. The older boys enjoyed playing hockey.

Mr. Charles found home life almost intolerable with teenage boys he didn't want. He asked Mrs. Charles to place the boys in a foster home and she refused. He gave Mrs. Charles an ultimatum: Either they go or I go. So he left.

Mrs. Charles's unwillingness to turn the AFDC money over to Mr. Charles changed the economic relationship between them. Prior to AFDC, Mr. Charles was in charge of all money and expenditures. And although Mr. Charles called the AFDC money "additional family money," he had no control over it. The AFDC money changed the political relationship between husband and wife, according to Mr. Charles. He came to me seeking advice for this deteriorating situation. Although Mrs. Charles was invited, she did not choose to attend. Mr. Charles became quite depressed. Since medical help was available to him where he worked, he was referred there for his depression.

THE GRIPES CASE

Mrs. Swift, a widow, married Dr. Gripes and brought into the marriage three daughters, aged twelve, fourteen, and seventeen. When Dr. Gripes tried to discipline the children, they would tell him he wasn't supporting them and had no right to tell them what to do. The girls were supported by funds inherited from their late father. Their mother tried to keep her family life with the three girls separate from her marriage. She tried to insulate her husband from conflict with the girls by making rules for them—what they were to do and not to do—so that the

girls felt restricted in their own home. The household became two camps—Dr. and Mrs. Gripes, and the former
Mrs. Swift and her three daughters.

Communication between the doctor and the girls had
stopped; each accused the other of being at fault. When he
felt the girls were doing something he didn't like and he
told them, they responded by defending themselves and
telling him he was all wrong, or by just walking away,
leaving him feeling rejected.

This family came for help. It was suggested that they
learn to negotiate listening contracts. They decided each
person would get ten minutes of uninterrupted time to
describe how they would like the family to get along.
They then negotiated another listening contract to decide
upon their goals and how to achieve them.

In addition, each girl and the doctor would try a
getting-to-know-you meeting. The rules called for only
small talk—no mention of money or discipline. The youngest daughter who was interested in medicine used her
time to talk about the medical profession.

Since the girls complained to their mother that they
did try to be nice to her husband, the doctor was advised
to listen attentively for any positive feelings expressed by
the girls and to respond to them. For example, if the youngest daughter would say, "Sometimes it's nice to know
there is a doctor in the house," the doctor could say, "I
am glad you feel more secure with me here," instead of the
usual, "Then why aren't you civil to me when I talk to
you?"

Mrs. Gripes was determined to keep this marriage from
falling apart, and while the family never achieved the close-

ness hoped for by her, the girls did learn to respect her husband when he dropped his demand for parental status. He was not their father. He had to win his own spurs as their "friend" and then the girls did award him a degree of parental relationship. When the oldest girl was married she asked the doctor to give her away at the wedding.

The making of one household from two separate families was a long, slow process which required daily attention. Because the girls received no money support from their stepfather, they resented his attempts to discipline them. They saw themselves as a separate family tolerating their mother's new husband for the sake of the mother. They saw this man as a "visitor" since the house in which the remarried family lived was purchased by their deceased father.

Second husbands and wives who move into the residence of an ongoing family must be prepared to meet opposition from children who have already staked out this home as theirs. Before these children will share their economic goods and exchange services with such a stepparent, the parties, all of them, need to carefully establish a second-family contract which identifies specific expectations and obligations of family members to each other.

Differing Expectations

Marriage sharing and individual rights *need not* run a collision course.

Marriage sharing and interests *will* collide, however, unless the partners establish for themselves some standards for a division of labor, for sharing assets, for accounting for income and expenditures, and more importantly for sharing life's most personal properties, starting with a bed.

CHILDHOOD-LEARNED PERSONAL ATTACHMENTS TO LIVING HABITS CAN BE OBSTACLES TO INSTANT COMPATIBILITY.

A "roller" and a "squeezer" are as emotionally attached to the way they use their toothpaste as a "spender" and a "saver" are to the disbursements of their cash. Even two people with different ideas about how a roll of toilet tissue should unroll can quarrel over which is "right."

When the spotlight of intimacy focuses upon the day-in and day-out exchanges of marriage, even partners who thought they knew each other very well before they married discover unanticipated differences.

The road from the "mine" to the "ours" of a good marriage can be rocky traveling.

When Margaret Waring says, "We began to fall out of love not over any one thing, it was a lot of little things like the laundry on the back stairs—I never could stand dirty laundry not in the hamper—and the wet towels—who is supposed to pick them up?—and the dirty dishes in the sink—I know he says it is more efficient to wait until the sink is full, but I don't like the mess," she speaks for so many frustrated by household management differences, all negotiable.

Ideally, husbands and wives will learn to see themselves as invested capital in the marriage business and respect and enhance their mutual investments through better communication. Bargaining is one kind of communication. Differences between the partners which go unresolved for a long time create chronic friction and some partners become insensitive to the irritation. This unnecessarily diminishes the quality of intimacy in their marriage.

Because the commodities of exchange are wrapped in emotionally charged packaging, negotiation between spouses requires that marriage partners learn the skills of give and take, and settlement.

Couples can use a business tool to help them learn to negotiate their expectations. It is called the Expectations Balance Sheet. There are two kinds of balance sheets possible, one simple and one comprehensive.

The Simple Balance Sheet

A simple balance sheet should list Expectations of Myself and Expectations of My Partner. Under Expectations of Myself, note what you expect of yourself and then grade yourself. Do you carry out these tasks or don't you? If you do, write "yes" next to the expectation. If you don't, write "no." Do the same for expectations of your partner. Does your partner do what you expect? Yes or no. This should give you a pretty good picture of the source of the disappointments in your marriage, or you may find more fulfillment than you expected. This is called a simple balance sheet because there is no particular order or subject matter in your listings. They can be random thoughts about your marriage and how satisfied you are with it. It is the beginning, however, of an overall view of your marriage.

The term "balance sheet" is borrowed from standard bookkeeping procedure. Every business must make a balance sheet to know if it is making or losing money. In the same way, marriage partners find out about their satisfactions and dissatisfactions. This is all a simple balance sheet will tell you—satisfactions and dissatisfactions in a general way. *But* if you want to go ahead and do something about the state of satisfaction in your marriage, you might need a more comprehensive balance sheet.

The Comprehensive Balance Sheet

To make the simple balance sheet into a comprehensive balance sheet—this can be done by each partner separately or by the partners together—take a close look at each expectation that you listed and study it. Does it express an idea, feeling, or judgment about power? about money? about sex? about relatives? If after each expectation you added additional columns labeled Political System, Economic System, and Kinship System, could you place a checkmark for each expectation in one of the columns? If you can, you will now have an additional reading on the state of satisfaction in your marriage, a more discriminating one.

When you and your partner exchange your comprehensive balance sheets and study them, you will have a great deal to talk about. You have, by using the balance sheet approach, objectified your differences; you have removed them from attack as personality problems. You have labeled them marriage problems instead—perhaps you could call them conflicting expectations.

Five

§

Marriage Is
a Kinship System

Of all my wife's relations,
I like myself the best.
Bob Hope

The husband-wife pair is the primary kinship unit. Through them the bonds of "in-lawship" are established. Relatives by blood and relatives by affinity make up the kinship. In some families the bonds of kinship are strong. Not so in others. Kinship expectations can create confusion in a new marriage. Often husbands and wives misinterpret attitudes toward kinship ties. For some, birthdays are cause for family celebrations; for others, birthdays are unimportant. Many buckets of tears have been spilled needlessly over birthday and anniversary celebrations. Kinship ritual experiences must be communicated time and time again. Ritualistic Sunday dinners are part of the kinship system for some partners. A husband who never attached importance to a birthday might not remember a wedding anniversary and could be accused of "lack of affection." A wife who refuses to go to her mother-in-law's for Sunday dinner could be called "selfish."

Kinship system ignorance can only be improved through more marriage work.

Relatives

Husband, wife, father, mother, child, sister, brother, grandfather, grandmother, grandchild, uncle, aunt, mother-in-law, father-in-law, brother-in-law, sister-in-law—these are the names we give to people who have special kinship ties. Every society has customs or laws that tell its citizens who are the specific persons—the kin—to whom you can turn for family ceremonies of birth, marriage, and death. Kin are the persons from whom you expect material aid and emotional support in case of trouble.

Husbands and Wives

The husband-wife pair is the foundation of the kinship network. In many societies custom teaches the young people everything they need to know about being a husband-wife pair. So fluid and unstructured is this pairing in our society, that married couples need *clues* to recognize kinship trouble and then, recognizing it, to know what to do about it. As many husbands and wives have discovered, ordinary words, when exchanged between kin-related husband and wife, can have a very extraordinary meaning.

In the play *Fiddler on the Roof,* Tevya, distraught and

tired after a long and unpleasant day, comes home to ask his wife, "Do you love me?" With some surprise in her voice, she says, "Do I love you? For twenty-five years I have done the dishes, made the beds, washed your clothes, cared for your children, prepared the Sabbath—Do I love you? *I'm your wife.*"

Husbands and wives frequently ask each other for confirmation of emotional support—"Tell me that you love me" and "Tell me that you need me" are common requests. Are these only simple demands for attention or are they clues that something else wants to be discussed?

In a very "healthy" family, an intact family, a simple answer like, "You know I do," might be a satisfactory response, but it is best to find out if there is more to be said. Between husband and wife, requests for emotional affirmation could mean, "I am thinking of something you *did* that I do not like, something which I feel says you don't care about me and I need to have you *show* me by *doing* something for me." Between the spoken words the professional can hear a disappointed feeling of, "I have the right to expect something more of you."

Let us look at Mr. and Mrs. M, who came to the marriage counselor because the number of their quarrels was getting out of hand. Mrs. M complained that Mr. M was not "loyal." They had been to a cocktail party where Mrs. M, an aggressive, forthright person, stated her views on a controversial political subject to Mr. X, another guest at the party. In some forceful and descriptive language, Mr. X told Mrs. M she was all wrong. Mr. M, who was also part of the group, agreed with Mr. X and said so. Mrs. M said, "This is treason!"

She explained: "In the privacy of our home, I do not

expect my husband to agree with me. But when we go out as husband and wife, I expect my husband to be on my side, or at least be neutral. How can he say he loves me when he hurts me in front of all those people?"

Is "togetherness" in public places a requirement of husband-wife kinship? Obviously, Mrs. M thought so. Kinship expectations in our society are so ill-defined that husbands and wives (as well as other relatives) are continually trying to add the details to their relationships. That is why every day in a marriage is a different day.

Mr. M asked me, "Am I wrong?"

"Wrong," I said, "is a judgment that I cannot make. You must make that decision for yourself. If Mrs. M says she expects this kind of solidarity between you and her, that is her definition of the marriage bond. If you have a different one, you have to find some way of resolving the difference."

Mr. M said he wanted to learn how to have a good time at a party, instead of another quarrel. Since he knew his wife frequently got into arguments at parties, he decided to talk with her before they went to the party about what he could or should not do to make the party a happy event. Through this decision he opened the lines of communication about party behavior *before* the party, asking for advice for himself.

He told his wife, "I have the following alternatives: (1) I can just listen and not say anything; (2) I can get into a conversation with someone else on my own; or (3) I can give my own point of view if necessary, as another point of view, not as a judge of your point of view or as siding with other people against you."

Presented with such alternatives, the couple had a good deal to discuss with each other. Ultimately, the Ms resolved their conflict this way: Mr. M began to let Mrs. M fight her own battles in company, since she really enjoyed the encounter, and instead of being an antagonist of his wife, he became an observer. Yet not every couple resolves this problem of "loyalty." Many husbands and wives continue to have disagreements about "presenting a solid front" all during their marriage.

Related to the "Let's present a solid front" attitude is the "Other people judge me by you" complaint. I have listened to wives tell how awful they felt at parties where their husbands drank too much, as though being married required the wife to control how much liquor her husband drank. Marriage to these wives means, "I am responsible for your social behavior, and if you are foolish, it is my fault." This is how Mrs. Pool saw it: "Every time we go to a party his tongue is way ahead of his head, and I am embarrassed." Mr. Pool, a banker, well-liked and respected in the community, says, "Sure, I have a few drinks and I have a good time. Everybody knows me and we are all friends."

My suggestion to Mrs. Pool was to take the attitude that people at the party do not hold her responsible for her husband's drinking. "If you feel yourself thinking, 'I am responsible for him,' try to remember you can be responsible *only* for yourself."

Mrs. Pool replied that intellectually she heard everything I said, but trying to feel that way is difficult. Did I have any other suggestions for her? "Sometimes it helps" I told her, "to make a comment to the other guests like, 'My husband is having a good time.' That tells the others you too are observing and just accepting the incident like any other guest."

Another party experience is the husband or wife (but more usually the husband) who falls asleep. A wife will say to her husband, "If you loved me you wouldn't fall asleep and embarrass me at the party." Should the wife wake the husband up? Is she responsible for her husband's sleeping at a party?

My advice to wives in this situation is: You can choose to ignore the whole thing or, if the hostess or someone else calls it to your attention, you can say, "I hope he is having a good time." I don't think it is the wife's duty to wake her husband. If he feels comfortable enough at the party to fall asleep, that is his choice. Social visiting is important to a good family life. It is the custom in our society to invite "the married couple," and although once at the party the sleeping husband might be called "not too sociable," I believe it is his presence there, and not how he performs as a guest, that should be the concern of the wife.

Another common complaint between husbands and wives is "failure to communicate," or in their words, "We have nothing to talk about, or if we start to talk about something, it soon goes dead—why?"

Listen to Mr. S during one of my interviews with the Ss. "When I come home from work and tell my wife that I bumped into Fred on the street, I don't want to be interrogated or cross-examined with 'What did you talk about? Did he say anything about . . . " or 'Why didn't you ask him . . . ?' She spoils the fun of my telling her that I even saw a person. I am just making small talk with her and she changes it into an inquisition."

Mrs. S, in a defensive voice, says, "He never talks to me." At this point in the interview I intervened. To Mrs. S I said, "You feel that when you are asking questions, you are carrying on a conversation?" Mr. S interjects, "Constant questioning is not a conversation."

"Tell your husband what you were trying to say to him by your questions," I suggested.

"I want to ask him what he did during the day," says Mrs. S.

Mr. S: "That's it! She doesn't want to tell me anything, she just wants to ask a bunch of questions."

Mrs. S recognized her dilemma. She wanted to be a part of her husband's life when he wasn't home—his office life and his daily life away from home. How was this possible without asking questions?

In fact, one might ask, what is *wrong* with asking questions? The only thing wrong with asking questions, in this particular case, is that Mr. S, for some reason, is annoyed by the questions. He is annoyed by the relationship established between the person who asks the questions and the person who answers. He feels uncomfortable in the presence of the questions asked by his wife. He hears an assumption of an attitude like, "I have the right to know."

Some people might be upset by Mr. S's attitude and say, "That's too bad. Does his wife have to be careful about the way she talks to her husband?"

The answer to that question is, yes, Mrs. S must be careful that she does not ask questions in a way that says, "I have the right to know." She might have such a right, if her husband wants to give it to her. But he has said that such questioning changes his volunteering information about the day, which he calls "small talk," into a serious conversation that makes him feel he is supposed to have answers to questions that never occurred to him to ask of other people. In other words, when Mrs. S begins her questions, Mr. S feels as though he should know much more than he knows in order to answer the questions.

What Mr. S is saying is, "I want to talk to my wife, too. I want to tell her about my day. But I want to tell her in my way."

I say to Mr. S, "What you are saying to me is, 'How do I get my wife to understand why I want to tell her about my day?' Instead of your wife's asking questions and wanting to know all about the other people you met during the day, you want her to respond to you. You want her to say something like, 'You sound as if you really enjoyed meeting them!' Or if you conveyed another impression about your meeting them, she should catch what the meeting meant to you. By asking questions about them, she turns you off. You too want to talk to your wife, but you want to talk about you."

"Exactly," said Mr. S. "You know, if she had said to me, 'You sound like you were surprised but glad to meet Fred,' I would have something to talk to her about. I would have told her how surprised I was, because Fred isn't usually in that end of town. As a matter of fact, I probably would have told her what we talked about, because now that I think about it, we talked about Fred's new job; but her questions, one after the other, turned me off."

"What you are saying is that if your wife could learn to talk to you about the things you are interested in, there could be a conversation. Can you give your wife a clue about the kind of talk that interests you?" I asked. "You don't like her questions, and she doesn't know what to say. All she knows is that she wants some verbal inter-action between the two of you."

What I was beginning to hint at was the need for a *strategy* for communication between Mr. and Mrs. S. Must there be such a strategy? Yes, there must, if their relation-ship is to continue.

I turned next to Mrs. S. "What can you *tell* your hus-band, when he comes home, instead of asking him? Per-haps there is a way of talking to your husband which tells him something in such a way that he will be encouraged to respond. You could try, 'I had a great day today.' You might get a response that says, 'Good,' and then you might say, 'I would like to tell you about it if you want to hear,' or 'I would love to listen if you want to tell me about your day.' Your husband might pick up on your signal and be-gin to talk. Or he might say, "I am tired now. I want to be quiet for a while,' which would be his signal to you."

There was some irony in this situation, and we all recognized it. It seems strange to tell a husband and wife, "You want to talk to each other because you somehow feel a husband and wife should be able to talk to each other; yet both of you agree that the way you have been talking to each other is not satisfactory." But this type of deteriorating relationship is what makes a strategy for communication so urgent and so vital.

All of the preceding examples reflect on the same ques-tion: When a man and woman become husband and wife, how responsible is each for the social behavior of the other? Being related means you do have obligations to each other, but under the American kinship system a wife is not her husband's keeper, nor is the husband the keeper of his wife. The relationship calls for a delicate balance between husband and wife, for cooperation and for individual freedom. Husbands and wives, as relatives, are having more trouble these days, because our male-female values are changing.

Father and Mother

In a chapter on relatives, it might surprise you to find so much time devoted to the husband and wife. The husband-wife relationship *is* marriage and we are concerned with helping married couples to recognize potential trouble and to know what to do about it. Trouble can come from two sources: conflict between husband and wife, and conflict with other relatives, such as children and in-laws.

Again let us look at Mr. and Mrs. S, whose husband-wife relationship was disturbed by kinship conflict over the way they behaved as parents.

Mr. S said, "I don't like my wife to say to me in front of the children, 'Let's take the kids out on Sunday.' I don't particularly like going out with the children. But she embarrasses me and puts me on the spot in front of them when she makes suggestions like that." Mr. S said it was harmful to his relationship with the children for him to say "no" in front of them, yet he might not want to say "yes." He did not want to be put in a situation where he was competing with his wife for the affection of their children.

Mrs. S's definition of the parent-child relationship did not fit Mr. S's. If she feels parents should take their children out to places of interest on Sunday, she should discuss this opinion privately with Mr. S. The mother-child and father-child values are not always identical, and, of course, there are no written pronouncements on this subject. A parent who assumes to interpret the kinship system for both parents might be disappointed to find this an area of difference. Parental differences can disturb the kinship ties of husband and wife, who are also (but quite separately) father and mother. In the case of Mr. and Mrs. S, parental differences were the basis for much of their marital difficulty. In a society as fluid as ours, there are often great differences between parents on what it means to be a responsible parent. It was important for Mr. and Mrs. S on this issue to separate their kinship ties of husband and wife from their relationship to each other as parents of the same children.

Many marriages are destroyed when husbands and wives in their roles as parents are angry at each other over child discipline, education, the family car, personal dress codes, room cleanliness, and other concerns of parents and children. When husbands and wives stop talking to each other because they are angry fathers and mothers, they confuse two separate sets of kinship obligations. They are the same persons performing two different roles in the same setting—the family. Adjusting to the obligations of both roles at the same time is occasionally difficult for some personalities. And this means trouble for the marriage. "Trouble" can be defined as a breakdown in communication. If one partner wants to try to reopen the talking between the partners, he/she can, I believe, be a self-counselor and can use the listening contract to reopen a talking relationship with his or her spouse, which is, of course, the primary kinship unit in the family. If either one begins with, "*I* have a problem, and *I* would like to work on it; I believe I could help myself better if I could enlist your help," renegotiation is on the way.

Most people like being asked to help. To be needed gives life meaning. In a marriage especially, where one partner says, "I need help," some quality with which all human beings are born, for which I have no name, seems to come forward and extend itself to the one in need. In my long experience, I have rarely seen a request for help denied. What happens sometimes is that the help is offered with conditions, the total of which may not be immediately acceptable. But if the feeling of wanting to help can be accepted and responded to by the person seeking help, then the partners are on their way to a communication experience. The next step is to establish the listening contract. Included in this listening contract should be agreed-upon "interrupters," if the partners find old wounds and anger creeping into the present discussions.

The example of Mr. and Mrs. S, necessarily brief in a book of this nature, is only to alert the reader to the *category* of mother-father kinship as a possible source of marital trouble.

The following section on in-laws will also, of necessity, be much briefer than it might be, since whole books could be written on the in-law relationship in the United States.

Again, my purpose is to help married people to sort out their problems into categories as the first step in facing a condition of hopelessness that says "everything is wrong between us."

In-Laws

Many societies have customs which tell in-laws how to behave toward each other; that is, they might have *joking, respect,* or *avoidance* relationships. For example, the traditional Navaho Indian mother-in-law wore bell earrings to make her whereabouts known so that her son-in-law would avoid her. But in the United States today in-laws, like other kinship relationships, are only vaguely defined. Many young marrieds spend quite a few years discovering for themselves whether to joke with, respect, or avoid their in-laws.

Mr. Black, married just six months, asked if he could see me without his wife because he wasn't sure that he had a legitimate complaint about his marriage. It concerned his mother-in-law. He said, "My wife talks to her mother on the telephone every night. I resent her talking to her mother when I am home. Tell me, Mrs. Kargman, is it wrong to be jealous of my mother-in-law? Am I wrong to feel my wife rejects me when she chooses to talk to her mother instead of talking to me?"

I asked Mr. Black if he had talked to his wife about his feeling of being rejected. He said, "I haven't even mentioned my feelings to her. I just read the paper and watch TV until she gets off the phone. By that time it is time to go to bed. I tried not to let it bother me, but it does, so I decided to find out from you if it is usual for married daughters to talk to their mothers every night."

What is the usual relationship between a married daughter and her mother? It is what every mother and married daughter say it is. The varieties of relationship are as varied as there are mothers and married daughters!

Mr. Black wasn't sure about how to interfere in this mother-married daughter relationship. I said, "You might tell your wife that you hesitate to talk to her about the evening phone calls she makes to her mother because you are unsure how to talk about them. What you do or say next depends upon whether your wife wants to engage in a listening contract with you. You might even tell her you were so concerned about whether you should discuss the matter that you went to see a marriage counselor first. Then, you might tell her that the marriage counselor suggested you ask her to listen to you talk about what is bothering you. It may be that after your wife explains to you what these phone calls mean to her, you will take another look at the whole situation and not feel like an 'outsider' in the mother-daughter-husband triangle."

Husbands like Mr. Black don't usually go to a marriage counselor asking for professional in-law advice. A more typical source for help is the newspaper advice column, or the television advice show.

Some current newspaper columns are written by psychologists, psychiatrists, social workers, and marriage counselors. These are generally not so interesting as the columns written by witty, newspaper people of long experience but no professional training, whose columns, on the whole, are adequate, but sometimes more glib than professional. Let us look at one letter and answer:

Dear Chatter:

Help! Please. What is the kindest way for a young married couple with a child to tell their parents on both sides to cool it? We don't want to seem unkind or ungrateful.

How many times a day should they phone? How many Sundays in a row should be devoted to parents?

These are disturbing questions and we don't have the answers. Do you?

Ohio

Dear Ohio:

No. Nobody has. It depends on a variety of things about which I know nothing. How often do they call? How long do they talk? Do they drop in uninvited? Do they invite you to their home or do they just come to yours? How long do they stay? Do they "take over" your child? Do you accept financial help from them? Expensive gifts? Favors, such as "sitting," taking the child when you go away on weekends or vacations? Does your spouse like your parents? Are they demanding, boring, tiresome? Or are they good company?

Every young married couple should sit down and think about these things and come up with answers that make sense to them.

And before you arrive at any conclusions,

please remember this: You will never regret it if you put yourself out a little for your folks. Most parents have put themselves out a great deal for their children.

Chatter

I believe that the young people seeking advice are, in a sense, asking for the same kind of clarification about our kinship system that Mr. Black was asking for—"Are there any rules that tell us what we can expect of our parents (or wife, or husband, or in-laws) and they of us?"

If I were to respond to the question, from my counseling orientation, my letter would look like this:

Dear Ohio:

You do ask disturbing questions. Both of you are thoughtful young people and want to do what is *right*. There are no customary or usual standards by which to judge the parent-grandparent relationship. This you already know, and what this means is that you have the burden of making your own standards. How do you know they will be acceptable? You say, how can we discuss this problem with the grandparents without getting into an argument? Your experience says it all becomes one angry mess that needs to be "cooled." First, a *contract to listen* must be established among all of the parties. Each party should have the opportunity for five or ten minutes to talk uninterrupted. You might begin (this is only a suggestion) with the introduction that you do want the grandparents to visit (a positive statement) and then you must be prepared to *tell* your plan. You state how often you would like them to call, how many Sundays you will give, etc. Now they know how you feel and what you are willing to give. After they have their chance to *tell,* you are on your way to a communication. I read in your letter an unwillingness to be the first to put down certain conditions. It is helpful to tell the grandparents what the conditions are as a starting point for discussion. Also, as a general rule, the persons presenting the problem usually have a tentative solution in mind, and if the social climate (which is what a listening contract creates) permits discussion to go forward, the problem is closer to a real and final solution. Good luck.

In Chapter Two I made the statement that every conversation takes place simultaneously on three levels: (1) idea, (2) feeling, and (3) judgment. The columnist chose to answer this letter on level one—the idea. The answer says, "I need more information," and, additionally, tells the writer to "put yourself out a little for your folks," when the letter says, "we do put ourselves out."

The letter writers are asking for a response at the *feeling* level. The words "help," "kindest," "cool it," "unkind," "ungrateful" are feeling words; also, the writers say, "These are disturbing questions." This letter shows concern for the kinship disturbances between the parents and the grandparents and between the lines I read an in-law problem on both sides. The writers are unhappy. We can assume from the letter that they tried to be kind, reasonable, and concerned but that something went wrong. That is why they cry for help.

Another common in-law problem among the young marrieds is what to call the in-law parents. Some in-laws feel comfortable enough to discuss "kinship terminology" even before marriage, while other in-laws go through life without ever being addressed by a kinship term. If you are about to be married, try to discuss in advance what your possibilities are and avoid unnecessary marital conflict. For instance, if you know your husband cannot feel comfortable calling your father "Dad," tell your father in private, and perhaps your father and your husband can solve their own in-law terminology problem.

Husbands and wives come into marriage with long-established ways of relating to their own mothers, fathers, sisters, and brothers. Marital trouble brews when the new in-law (daughter or son) tries to change familial networks of social communication. When Harriette and Ted Congdon came to see me, Harriette had already been to a lawyer to see about a divorce. The Congdons argued about Harriette's relations with Ted's mother and sister. While growing up, Harriette never had any warm family life; on the other hand, Ted came from a very close family. Thus, when the Congdons married, Harriette took Ted's family as her own, called her mother-in-law on the phone daily and spoke to her sister-in-law several times a week. She loved going to visit the in-laws with the children on Sunday, but Ted was a Sunday sailor, born on the sea cost of New England, and he wasn't about to give up his Sundays to go see his mother and his sister.

Harriette accused Ted of not caring for his family and being selfish because he wouldn't attend his mother's birthday party on a Sunday, nor his sister's anniversary on a Sunday. She felt she was so correct in her feelings about what families should do for each other that she tried to stop Ted from going sailing by using techniques like planning family parties on Sunday on purpose and then accusing him of lack of feeling. The conflict became a power fight that spread into all areas of the marriage.

The Congdons saved their marriage when each one recognized that they had different relationships with Ted's family, and that there was no wrong or right way to relate to family members. Each person had to make a self-adjustment. Ted was so pleased to have his wife "off his back," as he put it, that he decided to come home earlier than usual on Sundays and participate more in his wife's in-law activities, not because it was right (as his wife had insisted) but because he wanted to please his wife. This reason, if he needed one, was acceptable to him.

But Helen Young had an opposite problem. She decided that everyone in her mother-in-law's family was foolish, including her husband, since they let her mother-in-law tell them all what to do. However, she found out that the kinship ties of her husband's family could not be broken by the daughter-in-law. When Mrs. Young married her husband, his mother told her how to cook for him, how generally to give him the things that he liked in the maternal home. She also told her son how to be a husband. This advice did not bother Mr. Young, who had been relating this way to his mother for a long time—just listening, and then doing what he wanted.

But one day, Mrs. Young decided that her mother-in-law got away with too much and she "told her off." She really expected everyone to be pleased with her because no one else had told this woman how high-handed she was. Today Mrs. Young stays home while her husband takes the children to visit his mother. Mrs. Young has no family and is lonely. It seems she will stay that way until she can find some way to get back ino her husband's family without expecting them to change.

In-law problems that grow out of remarriage are becoming more prevalent. Our society is just beginning to accept divorce. We have not established customs for the remarried family and every in-law by remarriage is blazing a pioneer path.

In-law problems sometimes have special complications when the marrying partners come from different ethnic backgrounds. Let me tell you about Mr. and Mrs. P. When they first came to see me Mr. P was thirty-four years old; he had come to this country from Greece about six years before. He spoke English well enough to get by in the restaurant that he owned. He was a hard-working man and wanted to be an American businessman. Mrs. P was twenty-six years old, a very attractive blond woman. The Ps had been married five years and had two children, aged five and two. Mr. P met Mrs. P when she was a customer in his restaurant. She worked in a nightclub near the restaurant. Mrs. P had no nearby family since her parents were divorced and lived in the South.

Sunday was Mr. P's day off, and he wanted to spend it with his brothers and sisters and their families at his mother's house, where he ate all the Greek foods. Of course, everyone spoke Greek and Mrs. P felt as if nobody cared if she came or not, especially her mother-in-law.

Mrs. P was bored staying at home. Her husband worked in the restaurant six nights a week and she wanted to come and sit in the restaurant, too. But Mr. P said that was no place for a wife. He had very definite ideas about the place of a wife, and since he grew up in Greece, he had Greek standards of family life. On the other hand, Mrs. P had very little family life of any kind and would have preferred to forget that her husband was Greek.

When the Ps came for counseling, referred by the court because of the ages of the children, Mr. P was not comfortable talking about his family problems to a stranger. Eventually he and his wife agreed that this marriage would not work for them and they were divorced. Five years later I phoned Mr. P to follow up the post-divorce relationship between him and his ex-wife, and he told me he had married again, this time to a Greek woman, and was very happy. She got along fine with his mother and the rest of the family.

When husband and wife have different ethnic backgrounds there is a higher probability of in-law conflict than there is when both partners come from the same ethnic background.

For one thing, ethnic upbringing gives us our food preferences. I remember a young Jewish man, born and raised in Brooklyn, married to an Irish girl, who said, "If she would only buy a bagel and cream cheese for my Sunday breakfast, I would feel she loves me." Ethnic mothers-in-law feel their sons need *their* cooking since the wives have no interest in ethnic foods.

Also, ethnic groups have their family customs and holidays and expect all members of the family (those by birth *and* those by marriage) to participate. It is difficult for partners not of the same ethnic group to feel like part of the clan when the clan meets; instead, they often feel like "outsiders." My advice to mixed ethnic partners is that if the so-called outsider can accept the outsider status and can enjoy seeing the ethnic partner have a good time, the chance of having in-law trouble is diminished.

Can the do-it-yourself marriage counselor successfully work, without professional help, on relative problems such as those described in this chapter? I believe, as I said before, that every married person must try to counsel himself or herself. Each person must first venture a self-solution for a problem. It is true that the in-law problems and kinship problems discussed in this chapter are sometimes filled with so much emotion that quick anger and hostile questions cut off communication. But if you learn how to keep the lines of communication open, to accept responsibility for your own hostile questions, and to follow with a request to reopen the lines of communication using positive statements, listening contracts, and interrupters, you can be your own marriage counselor for rebuilding your kinship ties to relatives.

Six

§

Sexual Commitment

Doing What Comes Naturally

Just as new parents have faith that their child will develop and grow according to the genetic programming within all normal children, infant to child, so husband and wife have faith that they will learn "to do what comes naturally" in the most intimate exchanges of their total selves, physically, emotionally, and mentally.

The newborn marital couple differs from a new infant in so many ways that the metaphor must end here. For the newborn comes from the secure amniotic dependent climate of the womb into a closed family unit, either the married couple or an already existing nuclear family, and says, "Hey, open up and let me in!" This is where competition between family members begins.

At the birth of a marriage, a reverse process sets in. Husband and wife attach themselves to each other and feel a new oneness. They make their own amniotic fluid called "love," which protects them from the severe pain of improper fit of maleness and femaleness.

Electricians call electric plugs "male" and "female." Electric current will not pass through the connection unless the fit is proper. The "joy of marriage"—the energy of a successful marriage—begins with the creation or the birth of this invisible but very real new entity called the married couple or the new family.

Sexual Docking

Carl Jung, the psychologist, said every *male* is both male and female with a preponderance of the male because the sex organs are male. Likewise, every *female* is both female and male with a preponderance of female because the sex organs are female. Men and women marry when they sense they have found that other person whose mixture of male and female fits their own contours, not only in body, but emotionally and intellectually as well.

Marriage is the decision that docks the heretofore free-floating individuals into one working unit. In "docking," much like the space ships that rendezvous with each other, they exchange support systems which seem to be built to complement and enhance the effectiveness of each other. We have medical evidence to show that married people live longer and are happier than single people.

Until "docking" occurs, there is no way of knowing the degree of mutual contact or the efficiency of the energy systems. Simulated practice, like living together without marriage, can never accurately predict how the *real thing* will work, not in space and not in marriage, and this in spite of all the technology and experience in calculated risk-taking of modern science.

The three major connectors—body, emotions, and mind—work in wondrous and only in partially known ways. Some people dock with minimal adjustments. Other persons barely make it. But so long as the connection is sufficient to create a marriage form, there can be adjustment and growth if the marriage partners decide to improve their initial position.

Marriage Means the Right to Sexual Access

This new sexual unit called the "married couple" is established by the marriage contract, an invisible document in most cases.

Regardless of what the parties specifically contract, legal marriage in every society in the world recognizes the right of a husband and wife to have sexual access to each other. Sexual intercourse is expected in every marriage. When two marrying partners in the United States agree to live together without sexual intercourse, and if one partner should reconsider and decide that intercourse is an inalienable right of marriage obligating the other partner to participate in the sex act, then this right will be acknowledged in a court of law. While no court can order specific performance of the sex act, a court can decide that such a marriage is null and void.

On the other side of the coin, nonharmonious and unexpressed sexual wishes of the spouses may prevent the kind of "marriage docking" that both partners expect. Submission of sexual inventories of practices and procedures is unusual.

So, if sex is keeping your marriage from being what you and your spouse hope it can be, then some of the suggestions which follow may help you to help yourself.

Experimentation

"I never knew that taking a shower together could be so much fun!" Mr. Fled, age thirty-three, married seven years and father of Penelope and Jack, was describing a new sexual experience, obviously recalling in his mind some private pleasure as he spoke. He smiled and reached for his wife's hand resting on the sofa where both were seated. "Touching" was a problem for Mr. Fled. Mrs. Fled wanted very much to be touched, cuddled, embraced, and seduced. Mr. Fled had scheduled his evening hours after dinner with the *T.V. Guide* and he never went to bed until the eleven o'clock news was over. Because Mr. Fled refused to have intercourse with Mrs. Fled unless she showered, Mrs. Fled, tired from tending to two young children, four and two years old, took her shower at nine o'clock and was asleep before her husband came into the bed.

There were nights when Mrs. Fled did stay awake, or after a small snooze awakened, and when she tried to gently lift the top of her husband's pajamas to put her arm around his smooth, slim waist, he removed her hand.

Mr. and Mrs. Fled could talk to each other quite freely

about their marriage. However, talking about sex was less easy. Mr. Fled felt accused and he disliked hearing himself be his own defender. Why was he always defending? What if he didn't like being touched in bed by his wife? He loved his wife and was satisfied with all aspects of the marriage. If his wife was not, what could he do about it?

Mrs. Fled, besides being a very serious mother, was an artist. She was a graduate of the Museum School of Fine Arts. She loved to paint, decorate, sew, and generally be creative. She was adventurous and wanted her partner to "get out of the familiar rut," as she put it. Mrs. Fled commented that Mr. Fled not only disliked being touched by her, but said she noticed that "Father," her affectionate term for Mr. Fled, was uneasy when the children touched his face, especially if the children happened to have food on their hands. Mrs. Fled, who had been seeing a psychiatrist for about three years for her migraine headaches, wondered whether something in Mr. Fled's childhood was keeping him from enjoying adult touching experiences.

Mr. Fled recalled that his mother had a "thing" about neatness and cleanliness. He grew up always careful not to get dirty. He acquired the habit of protecting himself from being soiled by other children accidentally.

After hearing this, Mrs. Fled ventured the suggestion that if they both took a shower together, he could see that she was clean and didn't have to be afraid of getting dirty because the shower would keep them both clean.

Mr. Fled was accustomed to hearing new ideas from his wife. This last suggestion was not a put-down and seemed to capture his curiosity. "Let's experiment," Mrs. Fled said. "At worst, you can look upon the whole experience as one way of washing your wife's back. And other things might come out of it that neither one of us expected."

Mr. Fled laughed out loud as he recalled the soaping, slithering experience. "I don't even mind the children's gooey hands so much," he said. "I guess it takes a long time to get over some of the hang-ups I acquired listening to my mother. Perhaps I should say I just gave up taking my mother to bed with me."

Experimenting with sexual commitment is easy for some couples and very difficult for others. A not unfamiliar experience to many wives is a sudden change in a husband's request for intercourse. The word request doesn't adequately describe what takes place. A husband who previously was satisfied to initiate suggestive hints of interest once a week, signals his wife three or four days in succession that he wants her and needs her very much. This can go on for a period of weeks or even months. Some wives, out of a sense of duty, try to be cooperative. Some wives resist. And some wives, skilled in communicating with their husbands on the feeling level, sense that in their husbands' other roles as businessmen or professors or workers, or perhaps even as a member of a fraternal organization, or union, something has happened that has sent this husband looking for assurances and acceptance from his most intimate partner. When such a man is reassured of his wholeness in a loving sexual embrace by his wife, who says to herself, "he really needs me now," he knows and feels he is part of something more than himself, an indescribable core of support and affirmation, the stuff of which successful marriages are made. Whether the wives responded because they thought it was duty or didn't respond because they thought they were being used, either way, they were unhappy—and it is only by experimenting with being nurturing partners that could bring them unexpected happiness.

Being needed, even if such a need means giving of one's whole self sexually, is a compliment. The husband comes to his wife in time of trouble. He has many alternatives and chooses this one. Such a gesture as placing a troubled husband's head on her shoulder, if she had never tried initiating a comforting act before, could make such a wife feel very good. But remember, it is always an experiment. If the husband doesn't respond as expected by the wife, the husband didn't fail, the wife guessed wrong. The anger of disappointment, if there is any, must be directed at herself, not the husband. But disappointment need not be followed by anger. An intellectual judgment that the experiment didn't work will lead to new *ideas* instead of *feelings*.

More on Touching and Affection

"When he touches me, I know he wants to go to bed! No way!" exclaims Mrs. Ball, a tall, trim blond with Clairol tresses, while looking at her ex-basketball-pro husband. "Kiss me when he comes in the door at night?" she goes on. "I used to like that before we had children, but if I kiss him now when he comes in, I can barely fight myself loose to get into the kitchen and get the dinner going. I have things to do at six-thirty when he gets home."

Mr. Ball says, "I just want to give her a hug when I come home, but she won't even let me get near her anymore."

Reeducation for touching is what this married couple needs. A touch can be gentle or violent, can lead to affectionate feedback or hostile withdrawal. Where touching has become sexually negative behavior, then reeducation must start with an intellectual discussion between the parties about the concept of "touching." The goal should be: Let's talk about touching.

The marriage partner who responds to the statement, "Let's talk about touching," with the question, "Why won't you let me touch you?" is not talking about touching. That partner is talking about the other spouse, the "you" in the sentence.

Reeducation must start with a demonstration of "what is a touch." Whoever starts the reeducation process could ask permission to place the tip of one finger on the finger of the other. Here again, as elsewhere in this book, the partners must convey a sense of respect for the differences between them.

A new trust must be established, that touch for the sake of touch alone is all that the toucher intends. Touch alone, in an atmosphere of love, can have deep, sexual vibrations and joy. "Touch" as a sexual *idea* is a good subject for conversation between a husband and a wife. When some husbands and wives say, "What shall we talk about?" I sometimes suggest the subject of touch. Such verbal exchanges can help the marriage partners to learn more about each other's erogenous zones. After exploring the subject of touch as an idea exercise, the marriage partners can progress to the subject of touch as an emotional experience, exchanging confidences about feelings, including heretofore unmentioned wishes or fantasies about "touching." Soon certain kinds of touches—pinches, fast one-finger slides, whole hand squeezes, nibbling—all communicate their own special messages. Earlier in this book, it was mentioned that married couples over the years invent their own family shorthand. The connotations attached to simple acts of behavior, like touching, add to the vocabulary of this system of shorthand. So little can say so much! And in this manner, the wife who almost panicked when her husband tried to touch her before dinner, learns to talk about her fears and what to do about them. And her husband, unaware of the message his wife was receiving, learns to observe himself.

Unequal Sexual Commitment

A television viewer, encouraged by something said by me, sent the following letter:

Dear Marie Kargman:

Here is my problem.

I am twenty-four years old and have been married for two and a half years. I am eight months pregnant and very worried. My husband and I get along fine except in one area—sex. When we were first married all was well with sex—he wanted it quite a lot, and I always responded too. Then, after a year of married life it started dying off to about once a week (he stopped wanting it) up to the present of once a month. I have tried—really tried to discuss this calmly with him—he just flares up and gets mad and as a result when we do do it I am all tense and nervous. I have tried being aggressive with him in this area, but he pushes me aside and says he's tired. No other woman is involved either. I have talked the problem over with my doctor and he suggested talking it over with my husband which I found was futile.

My husband thinks I am making a mountain out of a molehill, but I really find this situation to be a problem. I know I need sex—why doesn't he?—I thought men had an unending drive for sex. I admit I need to be approached more slowly when having sex, and my husband climaxes quickly—as a result we have a problem—he's satisfied—I'm not and it's a tough situation. Could you please help me? I know sex shouldn't be everything in a marriage, but it is a vital part of being close. Please offer any helpful suggestions—I do hope to hear from you.

Sincerely,
Mrs. R

P.S. Do not mention my name on T.V.

Mrs. R's letter introduces a subject not yet discussed in this chapter: responsibility for sexual satisfaction in marriage. Volumes upon volumes have been written on sexual appetites, sexual cravings, sexual feeding, and sexual satisfaction. "I need sex," says Mrs. R, and continues, "I thought men had an unending drive for sex." Both of these statements are in the tradition of the mechanistic, animalistic, biological sex manuals which teach that the body is an object to be manipulated for sensation.

In marriage, sexual commitment is the ultimate in sharing. Where changes occur in the patterns of sharing between husband and wife, both partners are affected. A marriage, like all living things, is subject to change for many reasons, one being its own developmental cycle. Marriages do have patterns of growth and stabilization. The marriage described by Mrs. R two and a half years after marriage, is different from the marriage at the time of the wedding. She says the marriage has not changed, *just* the mechanics of sexual intercourse has changed.

But something has happened to the sharing process in the R family. The symptom for Mrs. R is an unhappiness that she believes is related to the sex act. Mr. R's symptoms are tiredness and anger.

Mrs. R's doctor, although well-meaning, cannot help her. She is, in fact, angry that the doctor told her the obvious—"Talk it over with your husband!" How do you talk to a man who won't listen? Mrs. R tried to talk about this marital problem, but the angry response of Mr. R, so totally unexpected by her, prevented her from continuing her conversation. "What has happened to your sex drive?" she asks her husband, as though to say, "Where is your manliness?" Mrs. R's letter says she feels very sorry for herself at this time of her pregnancy. She wants sympathy and it isn't forthcoming.

Lest the reader assume that the writer is hard on women because of what follows, it is imperative to repeat a fundamental of self-counseling: The marital partner who is seeking help must begin to make the changes necessary to improve the relationship. The partner who is seeking help is the only person available for helping. Mrs. R wrote the letter and the following suggestions are addressed to what *she can do* to help herself.

To Mrs. R I say, "These hints are some of those I might try. They may not fit your marriage. You must make that decision for yourself. Your goal should be to make listening a pleasant experience for him."

When Mrs. R asks, "Why don't you want sex tonight like you used to want it?" the question form infers the right to an answer and establishes a power conflict between the partners. Mrs. R wanted to discuss the *idea* of Mr. R's tiredness. Why was he tired? Was it to avoid having sex with her? Mr. R was rejecting conversation because he didn't want to be held accountable for his feelings. He would have liked to have his feelings accepted by his wife.

Listed below are some possible responses to Mr. R's "I'm tired."

1. Show concern for his tiredness: "Anything I can do to help?"

2. Ask: "Can I gently put my arm around your waist so I can feel close to you?"

3. Say: "I don't want to disturb your sleep, but may I kiss you good-night?"

All of the suggestions respond to and acknowledge Mr. R's *feeling* of being tired. There is an acceptance of his wish not to engage in the sex act.

Perhaps the next time Mrs. R tried to engage her husband in sexual play and he says "I'm tired," she might try,

"Let's not talk about sex. Let's just talk about how much I want to feel close to you." (No questions!) Said with feeling, there is a good chance that Mr. R will respond with feeling.

At another time, when they are not in bed, Mrs. R might suggest she would like to make a listening contract to *tell* Mr. R her feelings about their marriage and her sexual attitudes. As part of the contract she could say she has many questions to ask, but expects no answers unless he wants to give answers. She only asks to be heard. Mr. R might elect to answer or he might tell how he feels about sex during his wife's pregnancy. Thus each partner would contract for some *uninterrupted* listening time to talk about their mutual sexual commitment.

Sexual Gymnastics

The so-called Sexual Revolution of the fifties and sixties made available for public exhibition, photographs, movies, drawings, and live demonstrations of the infinite varieties of sexual contact possible between two or more human beings. I use the word "sexual" improperly, I believe, but in its popular context. To me, the word "sexual" includes more than contact just between the female and male sex organs.

The emotional and intellectual environment within which the male and female come into physical contact determines whether the activity is sexual or gymnastic. The Greeks had a word, *gymnazein,* which meant "to train naked." Many of the pictures and picture-books of the

Sexual Revolution show men and women in different stages of training. Some of the most popular books on sex warn the reader that not all of the suggestions should be tried unless the partners are in good physical condition, which means they have programmed their bodies to achieve some of the anatomical maneuvering required to achieve a position remotely resembling the photographs.

One very popular book warns the reader that perhaps "the matrimonial position" should be used for everyday sex and what I call gymnastics for "Sunday best."

Gymnastics can be sexual in marriage. Where both partners equally enjoy the sport, there is no problem. But where one partner is athletically inclined and the other is not, push-and-shove tactics create a psychological barrier for the nonathletic partner which often makes development into an athlete impossible. Not only does the body-fit begin to change, but the emotional and intellectual plugs deteriorate and diminish the flow of marital energy. The wholeness of marriage starts to crack.

Prevention of sexual deterioration is one way to prevent cracking. The unwritten sexual commitment which marriage partners make to each other is vague and open-ended. The partners themselves at the time of marriage cannot possibly know what their likes and dislikes will be at some future time. But they can set up some plan of action for whenever one or both of them "feel" the need for a more definite understanding.

Women clients have told me that their husbands, turned on by "gymnastic" photographs of nonrelated men and women, want their wives to imitate the women in the pictures. They want to play sex games, too. The wives who told me of these experiences felt these pictures did not express love relationships and were angry and disappointed that their husbands couldn't make the distinction.

If these same husbands would take the time and trouble to become teachers, or if they could suggest that both slowly learn together, as a new experience, small, very small increments of new sexual adventure, perhaps the emotional and intellectual attributes of sexual commitment would remain in balance.

Sexually Liberated Women

Today, married women are learning how to tune in to their own sexual wavelengths, to enjoy sex and experiment with partners in a way formerly reserved for some single women and men in general. Birth control and abortion have diminished the fear of pregnancy. Women are pursuing the athletics of sex with the vigor of "equal rights" believers, many feeling that sex as exercise and sex as part of the summation of an act of love are not one and the same thing. They believe they can love their husbands and still enjoy a special physical exercise with someone else. Men have believed this for years. And just as some husbands have learned how to teach their wives to be partners in the sport of sex, some women are now teaching their husbands how to be partners in the sport of sex. When this happens, neither liberated husbands nor liberated wives feel the need to seek gymnasts outside of the marriage.

Seven

§

Matrimonial Piracy

Kinship Interference

One of the most serious threats to kinship solidarity is a romantic interest, outside of marriage, of one of the spouses. Matrimonial piracy is not new. Ever since King David took Bath-Sheba, the wife of Uriah the Hittite, for himself, wife-stealing has been the prerogative of monarchs. But for the common man, the commandment "Thou shalt not covet thy neighbor's wife" was part of the value system of our society, up until the present. Is it changing? It seems to be changing and losing its sexist characteristics at the same time.

"Some say it seems to be a fashion among young unmarried women to catch a married man," said the "Fashion of the Times" (*New York Times,* spring 1974). But to wives and husbands who find their marriages invaded by "good friends," neighbors, and strangers, there is no sport in their personal tragedies. Even most states have erased alienation of affection laws.

Unsuspecting husbands and wives confronted by a declaration of "I want a divorce to marry someone else," are not emotionally prepared for a sudden separation. Some discarded spouses become martyrs and shortchange themselves by agreeing to divorce before they have planned for their own futures. Husbands and wives need time to shift from married lives to ex-married. But how can one partner ask for time when the other is in a hurry to remarry?

A request for time where a dissolution is due to third party intervention, is a plea for fairness. When Mrs. Gilla told me her husband wanted a divorce right away, I suggested that she say to him: "You have had time to think about leaving your marriage and to plan your future. I have not. You say for eight months you have been thinking about how bad our marriage is and now you have a solution for your life. Don't you think I need equal time? Is it fair that you had all those months and now you ask me to make an immediate decision?"

Mrs. Gilla's husband agreed that she needed some time to plan her own future. Would she work? What could she do? What training would she need? How much would it cost? What long-range educational plans needed to be made for the children? These are only a few of the questions to be investigated. And Mrs. Gilla also needed time to believe that reconciliation would not be possible. Mr. Gilla refused even to talk about coming back.

Not every matrimonial piracy ends in divorce. Some partners are able to plan new programs for themselves. In the cases which follow you will observe partners or just one partner, if both are not available, in the process of looking at their marriages threatened by piracy.

Playing the Game of Pursuit

Mrs. White, age thirty-two, mother of three small children, said her husband had been coming home quite late at night for the past several months. When she questioned him, he would say that he had been working late at the office and then the fellows stopped off for a few drinks and he really didn't notice the time. Mrs. White told me she noticed lipstick on her husband's collar but she didn't know whether to mention this to him or not. Other incidents, too, began to arouse Mrs. White's suspicions that there might be another woman in the picture. Cancelled checks in fairly large amounts made out to cash came back in the monthly bank statements. While Mr. White had always traveled a good deal in his job as a consultant, his traveling became even more frequent, and he was seldom home.

By the time Mrs. White got this far into her story, she was blotting tears, gasping for breath, and heaving sounds of despair that seemed to come from the bottom of her stomach. "I love my husband very much," she said. "He is a wonderful father. I depend upon him so, and I am frightened.

Mrs. White described their married life. Her husband, also thirty-two, was an executive moving up fast on the corporate ladder. She felt he was getting too big and too important for his own good. "We are living on an economic level we cannot afford, even though my husband does make a good salary." It was obvious to me from the tone of voice she used that Mrs. White was not happy with the way her husband was managing the household and she had conveyed this attitude to Mr. White in their conversations. Mrs. White was also unhappy in the new town to which they had moved, a distant suburb where Mrs. White felt very much alone. Several times she had asked her husband to go back to their native city, but he said he first wanted to make his mark in his present job.

Mrs. White noticed a decided decrease in her husband's sexual interest in her, and one night, when he came home very late, she awoke as he got into bed and said, "All right, tell me, who is she?" Her husband denied there was another woman and a quarrel ensued.

When Mrs. White came to see me she said, "If he would only say there was another woman, I would forgive him." Mrs. White made the assumption here that Mr. White would seek forgiveness. Since we did not know what Mr. White's attitude about the whole affair was, it was not fruitful to try to predict what he would do. The whole of counseling was concerned with what Mrs. White should do. What should be her plan to get her husband back?

Mrs. White, against her own desires, was involved in a competitive struggle for the affections of her husband. She thought she had won that battle when Mr. White married her; but somewhere during the course of their marriage she had lost him. It was difficult for Mrs. White to think of herself as competing with another woman for the affection of her own husband. She realized, however, that she must use all of her energies against a formidable foe. Her husband had fallen in love with another woman while he was still living with his wife and children. He failed to come home for dinner. He would give excuses that he had to work late at the office, or that he had gone out for a few drinks with a business associate and had forgotten all about time. Many were the nights he arrived home at 4:30 A.M. Yet Mr. White loved his children. On weekends he was a wonderful father to them. His children adored him. He still had some feeling for his wife and continued to sleep with her. What could his wife do? She wanted very much to keep the family together, and keep her self-respect at the same time.

"It is not easy," she said, "to watch your husband fondle your children when you know he is fondling another woman." She knew that pressure from his parents would be useless since his relationship with them was poor. She had considered, then discounted, the idea of going to her husband's boss (her rival, she suspected, worked in the same office as her husband). Her husband's boss could fire him from the job, but such action would leave her and the children without financial means. She had no money of her own. To go home to her family with her three children would be difficult and awkward. Yet, while she remained with her husband, life was extremely difficult for her.

Her husband had no solution. He knew he loved his children. At the moment he was uncertain of his feelings for his wife. His emotions were so absorbed in the illicit love affair that he had difficulty thinking rationally about his family feelings, and he didn't want to make any final decisions. He didn't want to seek psychiatric help, which his wife suggested. He wouldn't tell his wife the name of his love partner; thus Mrs. White could not try to reason or "bargain" with her as she thought she would like to do. Her alternative to fighting was giving up. She had thought about this too. Or should she ask her husband to leave until he had made up his mind which woman he wanted? I asked her what she hoped would happen if she asked her husband to leave. She answered that she hoped her husband would ask to stay. Was she prepared to be disappointed? I asked. She might run the risk of helping her husband to prefer the other woman. Many women have sent their husbands away expecting them to come begging for forgiveness, only to find they had sent their husbands out of their lives.

"What shall I do?" asked Mrs. White.

My advice to Mrs. White was: Take advantage of every moment you have with him to put your best foot forward. Talk about the present. When you feel yourself about to ask him why he is doing this terrible thing to you, stop! He may resent your attempt to make him accountable to you, and inwardly feel, "Who appointed her state's attorney?" Perhaps this is the time to review your attitudes of displeasure expressed earlier about his extravagant ways. Perhaps you were making judgments about finances that attacked his image of himself as a competent financial person. You might ask him if you could talk to him about some of your fears. Would he listen? Would he comment?

Sometimes an aggrieved wife will say, "Don't I have the right to feel hurt and wronged?" My answer is, "If you want to feel hurt and it makes you feel better to feel hurt, why not? But when you put it in terms of 'right' that means you believe your husband owes you something because he is involved with another woman." That kind of thinking can only lead to a contest as to who is more right. Did Mrs. White send her husband into the arms of another woman by her own acts? Or was Mr. White just weak? Looking for fault or blame is never a positive step in rebuilding a relationship. I reminded Mrs. White that since all the members of the family suffer when there has been an act of piracy, the assumption by any one person that he or she is the only one hurt and owed an explanation adds an additional burden to the already damaged relationship.

I told Mrs. White that what I was suggesting would be difficult. But since her goal was to learn to make each communication with her husband a positive experience, her own immediate need to be angry at her husband, while very legitimate and natural, might interfere with her more permanent need for reconciliation. I offered, "If your hope is to establish a new good relationship with your husband and you would like for him to say comforting words to you, then you must think of what you can do to motivate him to be nice to you—what can you do to make him want to see you feel good? If you do everything you know how to do, and he still isn't giving you the response you would like, there is nothing else you can do. And if you are disappointed, you will have the assurance that you tried."

Fortified with this philosophy, Mrs. White decided to woo her husband back. How? Instead of acting suspicious every morning and accusing Mr. White of lying about working late the night before, Mrs. White began to say "Good morning." When he said he had to go out of town, she said, "Have a good trip." Sometimes she asked if she could plan to have some friends in for dinner when he returned. She stopped being angry at him for going and no longer accused him of looking for trips just to get away from her and the children. Instead, when he said, "These trips take a lot out of me," she would agree that traveling wasn't always a pleasure and she learned to sometimes tuck a small personal note inside a shirt pocket, saying, "Hello from us," and relating some small incident about the children at school that she hadn't mentioned before. When he was home, she would say, "It is nice to have you home," and when she noticed he was trying to be nice to her, instead of her usual, "What did you do that makes you feel so guilty?" she told him he did something nice and she liked it.

None of this was easy because she knew the other woman was already considering herself engaged to Mr. White. Mrs. White came in to see me several times to refortify her decision. Eventually the Whites did move back to the city from which they came. In a letter to me, Mrs. White said the other woman tried to contact Mr. White even after they moved, but he said it was all over.

In the preceding case, since Mr. White elected not to come to counseling, Mrs. White assumed the burden of trying to counsel herself into a stable marriage. In the next case both partners came to counseling.

Marriage Disrupted By a Third Party

Dr. and Mrs. Exton had been married since the doctor's first year of medical school. Six and a half years and two children later, Mrs. Exton discovered that her husband, now a resident and almost finished with his training, was having an affair with a female resident and was unsure about whether he wanted to stay married to Mrs. Exton.

Dr. Exton is twenty-eight years old and his wife is thirty. His present job is for seven days and four or five nights a week. Since the demands of medical school and residency allow little home life, free time is in short supply and in great demand by all the parties. The doctor likes some privacy on the weekends and takes off on his bicycle. Mrs. Exton does not ride a bike. Mrs. Exton looks forward to seeing her husband and then feels rejected when he says he must have some time to himself.

Mrs. Exton is very pretty. She is going to graduate school part time in a library science program. For her, married life has been difficult, but she said she could now see the end of the line and was looking forward to the day her husband would end his hospital training.

She was worried that the end of his training might be the end of their marriage. He talked about wanting to be free to go camping, mountain climbing, and biking. He too was tired of the hard life of the medical student, intern, and resident.

Dr. Exton said he never intended to get involved with another woman, but on the nights that he was on call, he and the female resident who had the same schedule would sit around and talk. He just drifted from a casual social relationship into a love affair.

Mrs. Exton first suspected another woman when she smelled perfume on the doctor's body. When she told her husband she smelled perfume, he did not answer. She then *demanded* an answer and he denied being with another woman.

I am going to interrupt the story here to discuss this common situation of pushing the offending partner to reply to a question, when the asker already knows the answer and also knows that the whole situation is difficult and unpleasant for the partner. Here, for instance, Mrs. Exton already knew there was another woman, yet she insisted upon hearing it from the doctor, and since he wasn't ready to confront her, he lied. In his eyes the lie is excused because the emotional intensity surrounding the question made discussion impossible. Therefore, for him, it is better to lie than to create an even worse situation by answering. Also, Mrs. Exton wasn't really asking a question; she was telling the doctor that she knew about his deception, pretending to ask a question.

If Mrs. Exton really wanted to know something about the affair, she had the responsibility to communicate to the doctor that she was emotionally prepared to listen if he decided to tell her. But that was not the situation here. What she did communicate was the feeling that she was angry and hurt and demanded an explanation. This established a power contest which the doctor could not accept at that time.

Mrs. Exton was surprised to hear this interpretation of why Dr. Exton had to lie to her in order to keep the relationship from deteriorating even further. Several times she repeated, "I don't mind my husband having an affair, if he tells me about it." I asked her if she was trying to tell us she believed in "open marriage." She said she did, but she expected that in an open marriage her husband would continue to love her. In her case she was thinking of leaving her husband because he wasn't paying any attention to her and was neglecting her sexually. I asked her if she felt it was possible for a man to have two intense love affairs going at the same time. She said she had thought it was possible, but she had changed her mind.

The doctor said he owed "something" to the other woman. He had disrupted her life, and he felt she needed help and that he wanted to help her. Initially he thought he would divorce his wife and marry the female resident and they could do together all the things he longed to do. He now says that was like a fantasy, and he wants to stay with his family.

We talked about the doctor's feelings of responsibility and noted that they were admirable, but I questioned whether the doctor was the best one to help the now supposedly rejected mistress, if that was really his intent. Mrs. Exton wanted to know whether her rival read the doctor's attention now as therapeutic or as hope that his marriage still might end. The doctor said he would think about that.

In the meantime Dr. and Mrs. Exton began to plan weekends together. They went shopping for a bicycle for Mrs. Exton and planned to take outdoor trips with the children. They were able to have long talks about themselves and their future. The doctor, being a scientist, said he wanted to know why he got involved, and was this a one-time thing or would he find himself attracted to other women during his married life. I told him that questions beginning with "why?" in interpersonal relationships could only be explored over a long period of time. "Our goal," I said, "is to help you deal with the present, how to handle your day-to-day encounters; every day is an opportunity to rebuild. Some day you might discover the answer to your 'why?' by yourself in the course of an evolving husband-wife relationship. But if you want to explore the 'why?' now, I recommend you see a psychiatrist at your hospital."

Could the Extons continue to make progress at home? When Dr. Exton told of his plan to give up the other woman, he thought he was doing something good for his wife. When there was no response from Mrs. Exton, I asked the doctor, "Did you expect your wife to say something nice about your decision to give up the other woman?" He said, "Yes, I did." Then Mrs. Exton said, "I didn't know you wanted me to say something." I asked the doctor, "Were you disappointed when your wife didn't say anything?" He said, "I was." "Could you tell your wife you need a little encouragement—some sign tht she knows you are trying?" I asked. He looked at her and said, "I guess I could." Mrs. Exton did not talk easily. I told the doctor he could probably help her to talk to him. Mrs. Exton said she would like the doctor to tell her when he did not receive the response he had expected.

If the Extons continue to use at home some of the handles discussed in their office visits, they can rebuild their marriage.

Facing a Spouse-Theft

I once came across the statement, "No man can live with the terrible knowledge that he is not needed." When he first came to see me, Mr. Glass was living proof of this realization. Although he had noticed that for the past four months his wife was cool toward him, it wasn't until the day before he came in to see me that he asked her, "Is there someone else?" When his wife said, "Yes, but I wasn't intending to tell you until after Judah's Bar Mitzvah," Mr. Glass broke out into a cold sweat and began to cry.

Mr. Glass was forty-two years old. This was a first marriage for him. His wife was thirty-five years old, and this was her second marriage. Mr. Glass had adopted both children of his wife's first marriage, and there was a third child born to them. The family lived in a house Mr. Glass had owned before his marriage.

Mr. Glass was a taxi driver, but he was in no condition to work on the day he came to see me. His world was falling apart. Did he have to leave his house just because his wife asked him, he wanted to know. Did he need a lawyer right away? I assured Mr. Glass that he didn't have to leave his house and that there was no immediate need for a lawyer.

Mr. Glass didn't want a divorce, but wasn't very hopeful that his wife would want a reconciliation. He said his wife would go out almost every night and that she had decided to move out of the house and move in with her boyfriend. She said the children should stay with Mr. Glass until the end of the school year (this was April).

Mr. Glass had never had the care of the children and was scared. We discussed some possible solutions. He said his wife would come in during the day and do the laundry, and the two girls were capable of doing many of the household chores. I suggested that Mr. Glass contact Parents Without Partners and meet some other men who had the same problems.

Mr. Glass felt good about not leaving his house but was still very unhappy and cried a good deal. He had a tremendous investment in his marriage of eight years. Although during the course of counseling Mr. Glass was learning to cope with the children, he was having trouble adjusting to the rejection of his wife, and was questioning his own manliness. I felt he was going into a severe depression and asked him if he would like to see a psychiatrist. He was glad that I asked him, he said.

After a few visits with the psychiatrist, Mr. Glass felt better, and we talked about divorce, visitation, custody, and support. He decided he would wait until his wife filed for divorce to engage a lawyer. Now that he knew something about what he could expect from the court, he felt more comfortable.

After the school year, Mrs. Glass did file for divorce. Mr. Glass sold the house, and the divorce went through. Mrs. Glass now has custody of the children, yet Mr. Glass maintains a good relationship with them.

Mr. Glass, firm in his own mind that his marriage was over, showed very little curiosity about the man who was replacing him. He, instead, was concerned with his own next step. In the White and Exton cases, both women wanted to know more about the other woman, but neither made contact with her. In the case of Mr. and Mrs. Flat which follows, Mrs. Flat knew "the other woman"; they were good friends and saw each other as couples.

The Friendly Spouse-Stealer

Mr. and Mrs. Flat met when they both worked in the same office. Even though Mr. Flat was married at that time, they began to date. Eventually Mr. Flat divorced his wife and married the present Mrs. Flat. Six and a half years and two children later, the Flats were sitting in my office, discussing a possible divorce or reconciliation.

The problem? There was another woman in their lives—Lorna, Mr. Flat's secretary, a married mother of three children.

Lorna's husband was recently transferred to another city, and he had gone ahead to find housing for his family.

Mrs. Flat asked Mr. Flat to give up Lorna. He said he would try, but wanted to do it in his own way, gradually. At first Mrs. Flat agreed that she would share him with Lorna and they made a plan. Then Mrs. Flat was dissatisfied and asked Mr. Flat to see a marriage counselor with her.

Mrs. Flat told me she expected me to tell her husband to stop seeing Lorna. I said to her, "You say your husband doesn't listen to anyone, why do you think he will listen to me?" Mr. Flat, who was present at this meeting, said, "I really didn't want to come to a marriage counselor, but now I am glad that I came." He had many complaints about his wife, especially her "know-it-all attitude." But, he said, he would reconsider if he could be convinced that staying married would be best for the children.

Mrs. Flat, unhappy that the counseling wasn't going according to some idea she had, decided to try in her own way to deal with Lorna. First, she telephoned Lorna's husband to enlist his support. She was surprised when he said, "If my wife wants a divorce, I don't think I will stand in her way."

Then she decided to reason with Lorna. She called her on the telephone several times and wanted to meet with her, but Lorna refused and said, "I never intended to take your husband from you, it just happened that way."

Alone on a Saturday night, and desperate, she called her husband at Lorna's house to remind him that he had at one time said he would arrange a meeting between Lorna and the two of them, and could he do that *now*—this evening? He told her to meet him and Lorna in the supermarket parking lot. When she arrived there, Mr. Flat asked her to come into the backseat. As soon as Mrs. Flat attacked Lorna, calling her a husband-stealer, Mr. Flat asked her to leave, said their marriage was over, and that he was going to marry Lorna.

Monday morning Mrs. Flat came crying to my office, saying, "I think I need a psychiatrist." Everything she had tried had failed. And even though I had warned her that a triangle meeting would be a difficult task for her, she said she had needed to try it. She could use some psychiatric help and I referred her to a psychiatrist.

One year later, I phoned Mrs. Flat to ask how things were going. She was still in psychotherapy. And her marriage? Well, although her husband did not have grounds for divorce and she had not wanted to file for a divorce, her husband had cut off her bank account, taken her car away, not paid the taxes on the house, and made life so difficult that she did finally ask for the divorce. "And the children," I asked, "how are they?" "My youngest still keeps telling me, 'If you will be nice to Daddy, maybe he will come home, Mommy.'"

I think of Mrs. Flat as a person who could not be her own marriage counselor because she was psychologically unable to deal with the present without attacking her husband. Her husband had entered into a relationship which he was considering in terms of his future. But Mrs. Flat could not wait for Mr. Flat to try to work out a plan for himself—her own personality required her to be in control.

In the next case we see two parents placing their obligations to their children above their individual needs.

Is the Decision Mine?

Some people come to a marriage counselor to explore their alternatives, and having done this, they discontinue counseling to work it out on their own. Such a couple was Professor and Mrs. Knoll. Mrs. Knoll had fallen in love with another man and wanted her freedom. Professor Knoll said she could have her freedom but not their children. The professor still loved his wife and would not give up willingly, but since he knew he couldn't force her to stay, and since he enjoyed the family life they had, he did not interfere with her comings and goings.

If you would like to know what happened, here is the story in Mrs. Knoll's words. Although the Knolls came in to see me in the late sixties, for the purposes of this book I contacted Mrs. Knoll, the partner who had wanted to leave the marriage, seven years later. "What is your book about?," she asked. "About being your own marriage counselor," I responded. "That is exactly what we have been doing," she said, and sent me the following to be used in the book.

In 1967 I was thirty-two years old, the mother of two very young boys, the full-time editor of publications in a large corporation, the wife of a successful professor whom ten years before I had relentlessly pursued from the library stacks to the altar, and—suddenly—a mistress.

Q was tall—the first really tall man in my life—a self-made millionaire, an engineer who talked an awesome jargon in telephone calls that reached halfway around the world, and such an accomplished Don Juan he positively stunned me out of a monogamy I had never, never questioned. I admired his taste in women—his wife was my best friend.

In contrast, Jonathan, my husband, was predictable. I knew when he was in the kitchen drinking milk from the bottle, how long each morning he would read the newspaper, that at dinner parties he was sure to fall asleep in his chair. "What a rock," friends told me. Until I met Q I took it as a compliment. But in the summer of 1967, I suddenly felt my rock was a millstone.

The fall of 1967 was grim. We—Jonathan and I, Q and I, all of our relatives and all of us, and eventually Jonathan and I and a marriage counselor—went over and over the same ground. I broke plates, Jonathan hid our joint savings account book, Q moved out of his house (leaving behind not only my ex-best friend but their three children). Our two boys, then seven and five years old, reverted to bed-wetting and temper tantrums. The youngest developed an ingenious style in petty thievery, and they both grew increasingly violent in their play.

Eventually three things became clear: (1) Jonathan's and my sex life, always minimal and unsatisfactory to us both, was over, the end only aggravated, from my point of view, by his belated and intensely scientific interest in how-to-do-it. (2) Jonathan, advised by a brilliant lawyer who knew all the "tricks," would not let me have the children without the ugliest of public fights and the dirtiest of infighting (I, in turn, became quite messianic in my determination not to do the same). (3) Whatever it was that was wrong—and the more we talked the more there seemed to *be* wrong—was no *one* person's fault. For this invaluable insight, one on which I have patterned much of my life-style since the fall of 1967, I give full credit to the marriage counselor.

"It's broke," my father said in one of those endless conversations we were having then—all of us or some of us, I forget which of who, where, when—and so it was. I rented a nice apartment a block from the house and began devising elaborate visiting schedules designed (I thought) to conceal from the children the fact that their father and I were no longer living together. Q's wife began divorce proceedings.

Now it is 1974 and I'm still here. Will I ever go? Where will I go? Do I want to go? Has it been worth it? These questions and others like them have become my daily litany. It goes something like this:

Yes, it has been worth it. Yes, I may go sometime. I may even go with Q, who is still very much "the man" in my life, although we see each other so discreetly now that sometimes even we have trouble believing that it is for real. Or maybe I'll go by myself. Among other things, the marriage counselor tried to convince me how lonely Jonathan would be after our divorce, but I can honestly say that the threat of Jonathan's loneliness never entered my thinking. Jonathan is an adult and can take care of himself—just as I am an adult and should be able to take care of myself.

No, the sole reason that I stayed in 1967 and am still here in 1974 is the children. Except for the fact that I wish I had had the good sense to marry a different man at a later time in my life, I have no regrets. The children are my responsibility and my proof.

John is fourteen now, and Bill is twelve, and by anyone's standards both boys are terrific. John, six feet tall with a voice too low to sing in the school chorus, is a sailing champion with a shelfful of trophies to show for it, an expert skier, a qualified automobile mechanic, the star in school plays, a natural intellectual, and a tireless athlete—a winner who was accepted this spring at all four prep schools where he applied. Bill is, by student election and by his teacher's acclaim, the class leader. He is the "man" our neighbor leaves in charge of her house and dog when she goes off on round-the-world trips, and the one student in his class invited to everyone's birthday party. He skis all the difficult trails with his brother, and can beat us all in poker. When I bought myself a little sailing dinghy a few years ago, he was the one who taught me to sail it. He is his brother's best friend.

I am scarcely the person to cast stones, but when I look around at my friends and their children and assorted family structures, I wonder if children can reach John's and Bill's state of rugged self-assurance and good will without the bedrock of support of a stable home. This is a responsibility Jonathan and I contracted, albeit unwittingly, the night we conceived John fifteen years ago. As consenting adults, it is not a responsibility we feel we can abrogate.

In today's vernacular, Jonathan's and my marriage can probably best be described as a detente. Some subjects we simply avoid—sex (with regard to each other we remain celibate), his proclivity for the bathroom, my compulsive scheduling, and lots of others. In short, we have learned to overlook virtually all areas of personal conflict.

I'm not sure that if I were married to Q I would behave any differently. Who am I—or who is he—to impose my ways on him, or he his ways on me? We're both adults and don't need a framework of restrictions to hold us together. It helps, when the going gets tough, to keep a sense of humor. The boys are great—they can spot absurdities the way proofreaders spot typos.

Perhaps because we overlook areas of conflict to the point where I truly believe they no longer exist, Jonathan and I have become good, if wary, friends. We wisely moved to a new town, away from the physical reminders of some very ugly moments. We turn to each other for advice when we have business problems. We are both free-lance writers, and enjoy editing each other's work. We give and go to our share of dinner parties (where Jonathan doesn't always fall asleep, and when he does I ignore it). We make a fuss over birthdays, but scrupulously—dare I say thoughtfully?—avoid our anniversary. With the boys our lieutenants, we divide the housework right down the middle.

We do not hover over the children. Since we both work full-time, there are plenty of times the boys are home alone, and in the evenings we all have homework that keeps us out of each other's hair. At the same time, Jonathan and I put the bulk of our free time into matters concerning the children. We all have breakfast in the dining room together in the morning, and dinner there together at night. On weekends we ski, picnic, swim, and sail together, and our summer vacations are always a family affair. The boys have never gone to camp, and it doesn't look like they ever will. We have taken care, successfully I think, to keep the boys oblivious of our personal differences (they, in turn, keep to themselves whatever thoughts they may have about our twin beds). We have never once referred to the summer of 1967, and I honestly believe that the boys were so young then that without this oral reinforcement they have forgotten all about it. Certainly all of the undesirable personality traits they developed then have vanished.

Now what? John is going off to boarding school in September, and in a couple of years Bill will probably join him. I won't be caught by surprise. I have my profession. What then? At this point, Q, Jonathan, and I might all give different answers. The important thing to me is, what now? Now is still the children. This summer the four of us are going camping in Colorado—detente *in extremis,* perhaps, but frankly I cannot imagine a life without children—my children. I wouldn't be me.

Enclosed with the above communication was a letter which said, "Selfishly, I am grateful to you for this opportunity to think it all through again and decide once again, as I believe one must do, that I am currently on the right track."

Parent-Takers

Mrs. Knoll reminds us that "wife-takers" and "husband-takers" are also "parent-takers." What is best for the children of unhappily married parents is a subject for debate. Children can be flexible—like the little girl who asked her friend, "Do you have a weekend Daddy or one that lives with you all the time?" or, as Mrs. Knoll discovered with her own children, they can be very troubled by their parents' marital problems.

Other women and men have solved their problems in ways unique to their siituations. I recall the mother who moved into her lover's apartment, left the children where they were living with their father, but every day, after the father went to work, would arrive to keep house for the chldren and cook their dinner, leaving before her husband returned. She did this because she believed the children should not have to leave the house they loved because of her.

How to Stay Afloat on the Sea of Matrimony

1. Tell your spouse you want to do what you can to make this marriage work.

2. Plan new programs for yourself that you think your spouse might enjoy and invite your spouse to participate.

3. Believe, if you can, that psychologically speaking, your spouse feels already divorced.

4. See the other person as a competitor for the affections of your spouse and make yourself as attractive a person as possible.

5. Try to establish a listening contract with your spouse.

6. The partner who wants to reset the marriage must promise not to ask about the "affair."

7. If you talk about your competitor, don't be negative because your spouse will be pushed to defend your foe.

8. If you are not sure about the meaning of a particular conversation, learn to ask for a clarification, i.e., "I

am not sure I get your message. I believe this is what you are saying. . . . am I correct?"

9. Decide upon "interrupters" or signals which mean, "Let's stop here, argument will follow."

10. As long as you are both living together, use the time to rebuild.

11. If you notice an attempt to change, however small, say you notice it. Every change takes thought and should be rewarded if only by recognition.

12. Don't waste time and energy by pursuing "fault." Assigning guilt doesn't help to plan the future.

13. Use the listening contract for reintroducing and maintaining communication.

Eight

§

Nine Handles for Marriage Managers

Marital wisdom is inherited only by an anointed few. The rest of us struggle, taking one step forward and two steps back at difficult times, and from there on it's uphill with occasional plateaus. "Top-of-the-hillers" all agree that life on top is pretty special.

Rekindled feelings of deep affection improve with age. Marital wisdom thus prevents the misunderstandings that smother the flame and deprive it of the oxygen necessary for combustion. No husband and wife have identical definitions of marital wisdom; each spouse is free to choose any or all of the component parts of such a wisdom discussed throughout the preceding chapters, some of which are repeated below.

1. Separate problems you can do something about from those you can do nothing about. Discard the latter!

2. Attack the problem, not your partner.

3. Locate your problems in the marriage systems.

4. Change your marriage system. Accept your partner's personality.

5. Be specific; identify incidents of communication breakdown.

6. Eliminate competition, blame, fault, and accusations from your conversations.

7. Communicate respect for your partner.

8. Limit expectations, reduce disappointments.

9. Look for small changes.

SEPARATE PROBLEMS YOU CAN DO SOMETHING ABOUT FROM THOSE YOU CAN DO NOTHING ABOUT. DISCARD THE LATTER!

Each spouse must decide: Is there anything I can do to prevent further conflict? Energy spent telling someone else what to do is usually not well spent, especially if the person being told doesn't want to do whatever it is that is being asked. The spouse who says, "Why can't you make Teaser come home at a decent hour?" to a partner who already thinks their daughter won't listen, is asking for disappointment. Very often parents quarrel over who is going to discipline a child when they each know there is almost nothing they can do to make the child conform to the adult wish. All these parents can expect is to built stronger kinship, so that the child is motivated to seek a dialogue with them.

The daughter-in-law who *tells* her husband to *tell* his mother to *stop asking him* to stop by her house every evening after work is headed for trouble, since obviously her husband can do nothing about the demands his mother makes upon him. He cannot control the making of the demands; he can only decide what he will do about them. All his wife should do is tell the husband how she feels about his going to his mother's every evening.

It is impossible to have a happy marriage if your happiness is dependent upon what you want someone else to do.

ATTACK THE PROBLEM, NOT YOUR PARTNER.

Husbands and wives who come to a marriage counselor usually have reached an impasse because they each say to the other, "You are the cause." They use such language as "Why do you do these awful things to me?" "Why do you belittle me in public?" "Why do you stay out till early hours of the morning?" "Why can't you ever do anything I ask you to do?" All these add up to "Look at what you are doing to me—it is all your fault!" In addition, unsaid but intended, is a "there is something wrong with you" message.

All these partners would say, when asked, that they couldn't make a go of marriage because their personalities were so different. But this is a mistake. When a problem is in the marriage structure itself, in conflicting expectations, unwisely attacking the person ends communication and the talking stops. When one spouse says to the other, "You're stupid; you just don't know how to talk to your boss!" and the other answers with, "You're not so smart yourself!" the conversation ends. Personal attacks beget personal attacks. Whatever the exchange was between the spouse and the boss will never be discussed and an opportunity for husband and wife to share ideas and learn from an observed experience is lost. Very often it is the partners who attack each other who say they never have anything to say to each other or who use the overworked phrase, "We can't communicate."

We will find out what could have happened instead. But first, what did happen? The words "You are stupid," put into motion political forces within the marriage. Who are you to tell me I am stupid? One spouse has volunteered a personal, negative judgment that was not asked for. It might have made the name caller feel good for the moment, but it did not help the power fight (derogatory judgments of one spouse about another is a rank demoting maneuver in the fluid power structure) nor did it say why the spouse was so upset. Although some popular advice givers recommend that you say what you feel because it will make you feel better, they forget to warn you that if you attack another person your emotional release will probably be only fleetingly brief because the return attack may hurt even more.

Jockeying for power is a daily event in many marriages. Let me list some alternative ways in which spouse A could talk to spouse B and that would encourage the partners to talk to each other.

Alternative 1: "I don't like what I heard when you spoke to your boss." This comment by spouse A is power-neutral. There is no attack upon spouse B, merely a comment that is self-explaining: The statement did not please A. Every married person expects to be able to say what is "pleasing" to him or her and what is not. Now B can choose to reply to A on one of the three levels that have been discussed in the listening contract, i.e., to the idea, to the feeling, or to the judgment in A's statement. If spouse A is the one who wants to diminish power conflicts in this marriage, this alternative would give spouse A the opportunity to talk about the boss conversation and still avoid personal conflict.

Alternative 2: "Would you like to know what I think about the conversation you had with your boss?" Here spouse is defining the subject, the conversation, and asking if there is interest. As a general rule, when a partner asks for permission to talk about a particular subject, be put on notice that the asker suspects there might be some unintended negative overtones in what is about to be said but knows no other way to say it. Here the listener is being asked to only hear the idea and disregard the unintended feeling. The burden is now on B to accept this conversation on the terms stated, to be politically neutral. In both of the alternatives—and these are only two among many possible others—there is a respect for the marriage relationship, a desire to keep it stable, as well as a respect for the feelings of spouse B by spouse A. All "how do I say this without hurting the other person?" exercises are enriching experiences for persons trying to improve their marital happiness.

LOCATE YOUR PROBLEMS IN THE MARRIAGE SYSTEMS.

By focusing on the marriage problem itself—Where is it? In what part of the structure of marriage?—married people are freed to look at their marriage differences as something existing outside themselves. They can learn to talk about the irritants that exist in their particular kinship, political, and economic systems as separate from the way they have been affected by these irritants. The energies of the partners are then focussed on the problem they have before them: "What do we do with it?"

Couples need to learn that blame, fault, guilt—all past history with emotional overtones—do not contribute to the solution of a present problem. They must learn to use the history of their own family conflicts, not as penalties and punishment, but as personal experiential references. Here is an example.

Allan F doesn't like what he calls "the bickering" that goes on Sunday morning just before he leaves for sailing with his friend, Ben. They have been sailing on Sundays ever since high school. Since the birth of the couple's second child, Rose F has objected to Allan's taking the whole Sunday and coming in so late that she and the children go to Allan's mother's for dinner without him. Allan doesn't care to go to his mother's for Sunday dinner; when he lived at home he missed Sunday dinner. But Sunday dinner is important to Rose because she wants her children to know and love their grandparents. Allan, objecting at first to giving in to his wife's demands, changed his mind when he concluded that the conflict between Rose and himself was not a power fight (as he originally saw it) but a difference in kinship ties and kinship feelings. He decided he would leave sailing early enough to join them for dinner. And he has for the past five Sundays. But every Sunday before he leaves, Rose still reminds (he says "nags") him that he is to come home on time, that their day depends upon him. She also "reminds" him that he really doesn't want to come home even though he has promised to come on time. Allan says, "She can never forget the past, she worries that I will get too involved and won't get back on time—you know sailboats. But I am sick and tired of hearing about what I used to do. I *have* changed. How can my wife learn to deal with her own fears that I won't come on time?"

Originally the F's had a kinship problem, the Sunday dinner ritual. Now they have an economic problem: Allan F has traded some of his sailing time for what he thought was an acceptance by his wife of his right to sail on Sunday, but with an earlier return and a going to dinner. The bickering and the references to what he used to do, even though he has changed, makes Allan feel that his wife isn't keeping her end of the agreement, which was some peace for Allan.

In this case the kinship exchange created a new political problem—it established a new obligation and a right to expect. But it also provided an unbargained for reminder to Allan F from Rose F of their new Sunday dinner agreement.

They must now deal with their own feelings. Rose must try not to excuse her present worries because in the past they were well founded, but she must ask herself how nagging in the morning helps her and her marriage. If she decides that it doesn't, then she must find other ways of dealing with her fears. Bringing up the past is not helpful to her unless she learns to say, "I like the present much better," without talking about how awful those other ties were. On the other hand, Allan F's upsetness is for *him* to control. As long as he knows that he is going to come on time, and until his wife learns how to judge the present as it is, debating her instead of accepting her fear-ridden statements contributes to the bickering.

CHANGE YOUR MARRIAGE SYSTEM. ACCEPT YOUR PARTNER'S PERSONALITY.

Successful married partners learn to deal with the marriage itself as something separate and apart from themselves as individuals. All married people can learn that to change a potentially unhappy marriage into a good marriage does not mean they must change their personalities. Many people come to marriage counselors with a firm resolve not to change their personalities; they like themselves as they are. I say, "No one is asking you to change yourself. Rather, knowing yourself as you do, and knowing your spouse as you do, wouldn't you like to be able to talk about and resolve your differences?"

Partners learn that two different personalities can handle the same problem in different ways. This experience is usually contrary to what most couples expect, for at home, the common phrase usually is: "Why can't you change?" While there is no objection to any one partner's deciding to change, partners can learn how to work with each other, just as they are, to resolve differences located in the marriage itself.

BE SPECIFIC. IDENTIFY INCIDENTS OF COMMUNICATION BREAKDOWN.

Conflict, disagreement, argument is the subject matter for marriage counseling. In order to focus more clearly on the specific problem(s), husband and wife must see each other as engaged in some joint action such as doing the dishes, painting a room, or just talking to each other when the disagreement began. Spouses should be able to recall what each of them said, so that not only the facts but also the emotional tones in the voices and the judgments made can be reviewed. Both partners must be able to recall in their own minds the setting of the conflict: Who were the people present? Where were you, what place? Who began the conversation that ended in an argument? What was said? What was the response? What was the reaction to the response? Where did the interaction turn into a conflict?

If, for example, your wife asked you to help her with the dishes by saying, "Would you dry the dishes and put them away?" and you said, "Yes, I will," and you dried the dishes and put them in the cabinet wherever you saw space, and then your wife said, "My God! Can't you ever do anything right?" and you said, "Damn it! Nobody can ever please you! Don't you ever ask me to help you again!" and your wife ran out of the kitchen crying and yelling, "I can't stand it any more!" then you have an incident with substance to work on. You can ask yourself: "How can we have such a bitter exchange just over the dishes?" And if you really wanted to find out, and to help solve the problem, you could ask yourself, "Where did I go wrong?" and "What should I do about it now?"

The wife found fault with the husband's performance—he didn't put the dishes in their proper place. This was her message. But when she shouted at her husband that he didn't put the dishes where she wanted them, he responded to her "power" message with his own—What do you mean by using that tone of voice to me? After that exchange there was no attempt to talk about where to put the dishes, or about anything else.

After reflecting upon this incident, the husband did reopen communication with, "I guess I did put the dishes in the wrong place." Now the spouses have a variety of subjects to talk about, among them: How important is it for a husband to know where kitchen dishes belong? How should unexpected anger be dealt with in this family? Who should be the first to start talking again after an argument? In this case, because the particular incident is so specific in details, the partners can even choose to "replay" the whole event—reenacting the dish incident, making the changes that will prevent a breakdown, and testing their new skills.

Most of the people who come to see me don't begin their "tellings" with a specific incident and must be tutored to describe exactly what took place. Their complaints are generally vague descriptions of feelings and judgments (nearly always negative) about the other, about being hurt and always being wronged, like Dr. H who thinks he wants to leave his wife, Mary H, but before he does he decides to try marriage counseling. He tells me, "It has always got to be her way. I am sick and tired of being berated in public because she doesn't like what I say or what I wear. " Mrs. H, who came with her husband, looks puzzled. "Don't I have the right to differ with the doctor?" she says assertively. To talk about rights in a marriage at this point is premature. The spouses need first to know whether they are thinking about the same specific incidents, so I asked the doctor to give us all the details of the most recent incident that prodded him to seek help.

"I had just finished dressing; we were going out to dinner with some friends. The children were in the living room watching TV, and my wife was there too. I came into the room and the first thing I heard from her was, 'God! What a way to put yourself together. That shirt and tie don't go together—and they look terrible with the suit! I would be ashamed to be seen in public with you in that outfit.' Because the children were there, I didn't say anything. But when she started again in the restaurant to make fun of how I looked in front of our friends, I got very angry and just told her to keep quiet. I am a mild man and I don't like scenes in public. But she made me mad! She thinks she knows everything, that she has all the right answers." Mary H defensively answers, "Doesn't a wife have the right to comment on her husband's outlandish appearance? I just wanted my friends to know I wasn't responsible for how you look."

Was Mrs. H really asking what the rights of a wife are? And was she within her rights to make sure that her friends understood that she was not responsible for the way her husband dressed—and that she also wasn't proud of it? For her, being out in public together meant that people would judge her by how her husband looked, and she wanted them to know that although she felt responsible for the way her husband dressed, she was powerless to control him.

The H's, by reliving all the details of their last blowup in public, and recalling the words they used to attack each other in public, were each given the exercise to try some alternative ways of expressing their ideas, feelings, and judgments. The result: Dr. H said next time his wife comments on his clothes in public, and he was sure it would take a long time for her to change this habit, he will not comment, since he now understands she is trying to say something to make herself feel better—a public disavowal of responsibility for how her husband is dressed. And Mrs. H decided that if her friends say something about the way her husband is dressed, and she knows her friends do comment on clothes, she will just listen or, if she must, say she is not responsible for his appearance. Then they both laughed. Somehow, now the subject wasn't so important.

Only through paying attention to all the details of each incident of conflict does each partner learn how to locate where in the structure of marriage a particular irritant is.

ELIMINATE COMPETITION, BLAME, FAULT, AND ACCUSATIONS FROM YOUR CONVERSATIONS.

Marriage is a cooperative venture. Unfortunately, many of the attitudes learned in the competitive world of school and the acquisitive world of business are counter-productive in marriage.

Learning to give in at the proper time is very often necessary for family solidarity. It is a strength, and not the sign of weakness it might be in the nonfamily "outside" world. I remember Adele, thirty-four, mother of three children, married to Tom, a hard-driving business executive who was headed for the Presidents Club (an organization of corporative executives who make president of their company before age forty). She came to me in tears, to report how her husband worked late every night, how he never took her where she wanted to go, how he talked roughly to her in front of others and generally demeaned her so that other well meaning friends and relatives said, "Why do you let him make a dishrag out of you?"

And yet Adele was not truly unhappy with the way her life was, for she understood her husband. It was in fact her friends' criticism of what they called her giving-in behavior that had raised doubts in her mind. Is giving in the wrong thing to do? She wondered, until it drove her to counseling. After thinking it through, she decided that her so-called "giving in" to Tom was right for her—and right for her marriage.

Marriage is more than two people living together. It is two people living together with a common purpose and goal. Adele and her husband had that common goal—his success—and the knowledge of that goal helped them to live together cooperatively.

COMMUNICATE RESPECT FOR YOUR PARTNER.

A successful marriage is the result of painstaking care to respect one's self and one's partner; to take the time, trouble, thought, and action that will most fully tell the whole story behind a particular idea, or judgment. Too often a marriage partner carries on half of a communication inwardly, silently, and the other half out loud. I can tell by the movements of the eyes when a person has much to say on a subject, but remains largely silent making a single syllable response, if any. If I ask what the person was thinking about before speaking, the report can best be described as a debate with the self, weighing all the pros and cons and testing possible ways of having a conversation. When I ask: "At home, do you tell your partner how you debated with yourself whether or not to say what you did say?" the usual answer is, "No, but I guess I should have."

A partner who hesitates to say what he or she is thinking for fear that it might be misunderstood learns that sharing the inner debate is one way of telling the listener that you want to interact in a pleasant, agreeable way; that you are having a problem, and can the listener help? The more clues you give your partner, the more sensitive the response. Thus a spouse who wants to discuss an idea, such as why so much money was spent on a particular Christmas gift, and wrestles with hostility in the voice, could avoid trouble by admitting, "I don't know how to say this without sounding hostile, but I don't mean to be hostile, so could you try to disregard my tone of voice and just talk about the gift?"

Caring about how you sound to yourself and to your spouse is a sign both of self-respect and of respect for your partner.

LIMIT EXPECTATIONS AND REDUCE DISAPPOINTMENTS.

Expectations fulfilled make a happy marriage. Expectations that can be *self-fulfilling,* requiring only yourself to meet them, are the most successful kind to have. The wife who says, "I am going to ask my husband to kiss me when he comes through the front door tonight" (this couple has not demonstrated affection to each other except in the bedroom) and then proceeds to do exactly as planned, has fulfilled her own expectation. She expected to ask for a kiss and she did ask for a kiss. Whether or not her husband will kiss her is not within her control. If he does kiss her, she is even happier. But if he doesn't she is content with herself because she made the decision to ask and she did ask—mission accomplished. To herself, she says, "Look what he missed." If she wants to talk to her husband about front door greetings again, she can do so more readily without anger, since she didn't expect him to kiss her, only hoped that he might.

Talking about hopes makes for good husband and wife conversation: what each hopes that some day each will be able to expect from each other. But until their political system becomes grooved into reciprocally accepted expectations, there will be disappointments related to unfulfilled expectations.

Learning to deal with self-inflicted disappointments from unrealistic expectations decreases your hostility toward your partner. You can manage temporary unhappiness better when you ask yourself, "Why am I feeling unhappy; is this what I want?" Your feelings then become ideas for you to think about. Evaluating the success or failure of your own expectations puts you in control of those you wish to keep and those you choose to discard as being counter-productive to marital happiness.

LOOK FOR SMALL CHANGES.

Marriages grow in small increments that expand with encouragement. A small change—like doing a formerly troublesome task differently or expressing a feeling differently—can be significant for the changing partner but go unrecognized by a mate who is programmed to see only gross and total changes. Therefore, each partner must look vigilantly for his and her own changing ways of relating to each other and learn to talk about them to each other because when you counsel yourself you also look to yourself for compliments, for doing a job well, as well as hoping that your spouse will recognize your efforts to make the marriage better. By helping your partner to be more aware of your changes you help your partner to adjust the antenna in your direction and enhance the possibility of being complimented by your spouse. Each partner must feel free to say, "I think I am improving" or "I think you are improving." These compliments encourage the spouses to listen to each other more carefully, since they are pleasant to hear. It's easy to pay attention to words calculated to make you feel good, but only if you hear them. Again, if your own eyes and ears are not finely tuned to see and hear small increments of change, you might miss an opportunity to compliment your spouse, just as Robin Bell missed hers.

Robin and Michael B, after six weeks of learning how to be their own marriage counselors, decided to be their own. Two months later, Robin called, upset because Michael said he doesn't love her anymore. This announcement, part of a quarrel, took Robin by surprise because she said they were really enjoying each other. Here is her story.

All the while Michael was in graduate school, they used to talk about traveling after he got his degree. They were talking about vacations, and Michael said he would like to buy a house in New Hampshire where they could ski in the winter and swim in the summer. Robin saw her dreams of traveling to Europe go up in smoke and in anger said, "I like Cape Cod better." Then Robin, reverting to some earlier behavior that had brought the B's to counseling in the first place, began a persistent, constant stream of questions all beginning with "why?" Why can't we travel in Europe? Why do we need a ski house in New Hampshire? Why aren't my wishes as improtant as yours?

And Michael's answer was, "Go where you want, I just don't love you anymore!" and he walked out of the room, which had been his usual way of dealing with the previous "why's." In a few moments, however, Michael came back into the room and said, "Look, I can't take a week of silence; it doesn't help anyone. I want to go skiing in New Hampshire next weekend; do you want to go?" This was change. Prior to counseling, when Michael and Robin argued, and she "why'd," he would not talk to her for three days and by that time she would be depressed and wouldn't talk to him for the rest of the week. Also, Robin, who said she would like to go to New Hampshire, reported another change. Michael was not accustomed to telephoning her during the day, but the day after the argument he did call from the office to ask how she was.

Here were two specific changes, both indicating a growth in Michael's attempts to improve the marriage, which Robin failed to see and to note and to use for continuing the growth direction of this marriage. Because she was so upset by the declaration "I don't love you," she failed to observe such significant change, which could have helped her to understand Michael's outburst.

There was no specific house in New Hampshire.

Michael was only sharing a dream for the future. Robin didn't hear the dream; she already was fighting for her right to be heard in a major family decision. Michael, counseling himself, decided he would not let the old patterns take over, so he changed. But Michael had not yet learned how to deal with the repeated "why's" except to say what he had said in the past; that always stopped the questions.

Robin, her antenna readjusted, was now ready to tell Michael that she was pleased that he talked to her after the argument and she too was concerned about the "silent week treatment." She would also note, with affection, his telephoning the next day. They had a very good weekend in New Hampshire.

Robin missed Michael's clues. Modesty sometimes hinders such marital progress and Michael would have helped Robin if he could have said, when he returned to talk to her, I hope you notice how I have changed. He did try to tell her, but she needed more specific help.

Each spouse must feel free to tell the other when they feel pleased with their own progress. And if you would like a compliment now and then for your own efforts, sometimes you must ask for one and even tell your spouse which specific compliment you would like. In this way you learn that many happy experiences in marriage are self-made.

When husbands and wives compete to be right and to win, a tremendous amount of emotional energy goes into what I call "playing the game of self-defense." If the players are not equally endowed with the talent of verbal barrage, this game can be devastating to a relationship. The less verbal person soon learns the "I cannot win" posture and withdraws. Such partners, unequal in their abilities to use words as fighting weapons, need a mechanism to make them equal; they need the listening contract and its built-in warning signals, the symbolic interrupters.

But, even more important, when the partners learn to be expert listeners, tuned in to hearing the three separate levels of conversation—the idea, the feeling, and the judgment—the urge or the need to defend oneself from this verbal attack seems to dissipate, and each partner is prepared to go forward on one of the three levels being expressed in the conversation, instead of going back into a non-productive recitation of "why I did it . . . . "

Psychologically, a partner who is busy thinking about ways to defend has stopped listening. Self-defense and listening are incompatible.

And lastly, your own familiarity with the three systems in your family—the political, economic, and kinship—will help you to enjoy your own observations of yourself and your spouse interacting with each other, and with the important "others" who are part of your marriage. What at one time seemed like chaos can now be called happy order and fun. Knowing the three systems will put some peace into your married life and will give you back the energy you lose in power fights to use instead to achieve all the pleasant rewards that come from a good marriage.

§
Index

For Individual or Bulk Orders

Write to Foundation Books, 151 Tremont Street PH, Boston, MA 02111, (617-423-4958) or use coupon below.

Please send me _____ copy(ies) of *How to Manage a Marriage* at a cost of $6.95 per copy plus $1.00 per copy to cover postage and handling. I am enclosing a check or money order (not cash) for my order.

Name _____

Address _____

City/Town _____

State _____ Zip Code _____

Foundation Books
151 Tremont Street P.H.
Boston, Mass. 02111

About the Author

Marie Witkin Kargman, A.M. Harvard, J.D. DePaul University, clinical family sociologist and specialist in Family Law, pioneered the use of social system theory in marriage counseling. Her career spans thirty years in marriage counseling, divorce counseling, publishing and lecturing on the dynamics of family living. Chairing the first Governor's Advisory Council on Home and Family in Massachusetts, she introduced into the Massachusetts Legislature Bills dealing with family education for divorce litigants and their children, thus contributing her counseling skills, legal knowledge and experience in the public interest. Mrs. Kargman taught at Boston University for several years and from time to time lectures at Harvard University on subjects that combine family sociology and family law. She is known throughout New England for her innovative television marriage counseling programs encouraging live audience participation. Her name appears in *Two Thousand Women of Achievement, Who's Who In American Women* and *Who's Who in American Law.* Her published articles appear in *The Family Coordinator, Marriage and Family Living, The American Bar Association Journal, The Women Lawyers Journal, The Practical Lawyer, The Massachusetts Law Quarterly, Et. Al.* and *The Journal of Divorce.*

How to Manage a Marriage

"How can I keep my marriage from falling apart?"

For more than 25 years of clinical practice Marie Kargman has been helping couples to find effective answers to this question.

One answer is the Listening Contract: agreeing to listen without interrupting; to interrupt with permission; to express a negative feeling without arousing hostility; to ask for love and get it.

With the revolutionary advice to "forget psychiatry," Mrs. Kargman teaches clients to use the personalities they already have to "enjoy a husband-and-wife relationship that lives . . . achieves . . . suffers . . . rebuilds . . . and bathes itself in the balm of loving mutual respect."

Unlike any other book, *How to Manage a Marriage* defines the family as a social system with a mini-government, a mini-business and a kinship system, making the complexity of marriage more manageable.